Contents

Introduction

Dinghy sailing – a pursuit so absorbing that few people who take it up give it up completely.

Dinghy sailing can mean anything from a quiet evening sail along a rush-lined river to a thrashing, salt-stung beat on the open sea. It can range from a creeping, painstaking day on a windless reservoir, to a full-blooded reach, with the dinghy planing on the very edge of control. At speed, the spray sizzles on either side of the boat, and the excitement is so intense that you barely have time to enjoy it.

Dinghy sailing can mean cruising far afield with your car and trailer, or it can mean going afloat on your afternoon off. It can mean enjoying some not-too-serious competition at the local club, or it can mean months or even years of dedicated, single-minded work to win a national or international championship, or even to try for a place in the Olympic team.

Dinghy sailing is a sport with endless variety and endless possibilities – in the end, it is what you want it to be.

The Development of Dinghy Sailing

No-one can put a date on when dinghy sailing first emerged as a pastime, except to say that it grew partly from the small working boats that operated around the coasts of Britain and North America – in particular the north-eastern seaboard of the United States – and partly from the grander pastime of yachting, which reached its heyday during the period at the end of the last century and the beginning of this.

Probably the first longshore fisherman to leave his nets ashore and take his wife and kids for an outing in his single-sailed rowing boat was the first dinghy sailor. The sailing dinghy as a modern type, however, goes back no further than the early part of the twentieth century.

The Beginnings

By the 1910's and 1920's, small boat sailing and racing were already well established in the USA, Britain and Ireland (which country can claim the oldest yacht club in the world – now called the Royal Cork Yacht Club, founded in 1720). The boats used retractable keels called centreplates. In addition, crew weight and position played an important part in maintaining stability and trim. These are the two essential distinguishing features of the sailing dinghy.

Early Sailing Dinghies

These early dinghies were different from the dinghies of today in that they were developed and sailed very much on the lines of the larger yachts, whose activities they emulated. The crews sat in them, not on them; indeed in England especially it was considered both unseaman-like and somewhat unsporting to lean over the side. Centreplates were of metal, their primary function being to provide stability, in the same way that the bigger yachts derived stability from their ballast keels.

The Great Designers

In 1928, the face of dinghy design was changed by two men in England who raced in the International 14 class – Tom Thorneycroft and Uffa Fox. Between them, Thorneycroft and Fox developed the notion of the planing dinghy. This was one which, by virtue of its shape and speed, would be able to rise out of its displacement mode and lift on to its own bow wave, skimming along the surface of the water rather than ploughing through it.

Avenger

Avenger, an International 14 designed, built and sailed by Uffa Fox in the British season of 1928, became perhaps the most famous dinghy of all time, and the first true planing dinghy. Before that time, dinghies had been known to plane in the way that powered speedboats of the time could plane, but this was seen only as a phenomenon, a rarity.

Avenger was the first dinghy to be designed to plane under normal sailing conditions, and also to have a good windward performance. In 57 starts in the 1928 season, *Avenger* won 52 races, came second in two others, and third in the remaining three – a remarkable record.

The characteristics developed in *Avenger* were soon exploited by other designers and in other classes, and the day of the planing sailing dinghy had arrived.

The United States
In the USA, interest in small boat sailing had grown enormously in the Twenties and Thirties, not least thanks to the influence of a hugely successful magazine called *The Rudder*. *The Rudder* often published the designs of new boats that were capable of being built by amateurs in their own homes.

Two such designs were the *Lightning* and the *Snipe*, both of which were built in tens of thousands, and both of which are still being built and raced today.

In contrast to British racing dinghies of the time, these US designs were of hard-chine, almost box-like construction for ease of amateur building. By contrast, before the Second World War, virtually all British sailing dinghies were designed to be built by professional boatbuilders, using traditional methods and techniques.

Plywood Dinghies
By a strange twist of fate, the Second World War gave to dinghy sailing a material of enormous benefit – plywood, or to be more precise, marine grade plywood, made with glues suitable for use in the hostile environment of sea water. Before the war there had been plywood available that was suitable for the manufacture of, for example, tea chests. However, it was during the acute wartime metal shortages that plywoods suitable for aircraft construction were developed. When the fighting was over, these tools of war became the means of an enormous expansion in dinghy sailing.

Before the war, dinghies on both sides of the Atlantic had been built of solid timber. During and immediately after the war, timber suitable for boat building was in very short supply, especially in Britain. However, the increasing availability of plywood soon overcame this shortage. Not only that, but building in plywood was much easier than traditional methods of planked construction, and as wartime restrictions and austerities eased, the great do-it-yourself dinghy boom began.

The Boom Years
The dinghy boom was fuelled by increasing affluence, and greater leisure time among those who had never before given much thought to the idea of 'going yachting'. They were aided by the lifting of the veil of mystique which had hung over traditional dinghy building in the prewar, pre-plywood era, and by the proliferation of designs suitable for building in the new materials and by the new methods.

Most prolific of the new designers was Jack Holt, an Englishman based in London who with his American partner Beecher Moore (who also lived in London) was responsible for many of the now world-wide dinghy designs of this era: the Enterprise, the GP 14, and the Cadet. Other designers were at work on dinghies that could be assembled at home.

A Jack Holt-designed GP14, classic product of the dinghy sailing boom.

Glassfibre

The 1950's saw an enormous expansion in the sport of dinghy sailing, and just as the momentum which this provided was beginning to slow down, there arrived yet another development to keep things going – glassfibre.

Glassfibre – or to give it its proper but somewhat clumsy name, glass-reinforced-plastic – arrived on the scene just as enthusiasm for home dinghy building was beginning to wane in the garages and spare rooms of Britain.

The Consumer Era was now in full swing, and people preferred and had the money to buy rather than make: mass-production of sailing dinghies became possible, while at the same time the greater versatility of glassfibre freed dinghy design from the constraints which designing for plywood home-building had placed upon shape and hull form in particular.

A new generation of designs, produced specifically for glassfibre production, now came into being, while many of the older and better-established designs adopted glassfibre construction to prevent themselves from becoming outmoded.

Decline

Yet while the advent of glassfibre opened another new era in dinghy sailing, it also dealt the sport a severe blow, for it made possible the development of the small relatively cheap, mass-produced yacht.

Many of those who had come to dinghy sailing in the Fifties and Sixties were, by the mid to late Seventies, not just older, but also financially better off. While such people 'moved up' from dinghy sailing to yachting, there were fewer youngsters to take up dinghy sailing – not least because of the availability of so many alternative forms of leisure activity, from mountaineering to disco dancing.

By the late Seventies, dinghy sailing was undergoing an undeniable decline, which was accelerated by the worsening economic and business climate all over Europe and America. In Britain and the USA, growth of the pastime all but stopped, and dinghy manufacturers, like so many others in the leisure industry, had a lean time of it.

Dinghy Sailing Today

By the early 1980's, dinghy sailing was once again increasing in popularity. A measure of this renaissance has been the increase in the number of television programmes devoted to watersports. In Britain, the Royal Yachting Association has reported a marked increase in the number of people taking basic dinghy sailing courses.

Ironically, a major influence has been the phenomenal growth and development of windsurfing. In the same way as the dinghy boom of the Fifties, the windsurfing boom of the Seventies and Eighties introduced watersports to a whole new generation. Many such people, having had their first taste of sailing on a board, perhaps on holiday, have transferred their allegiance to dinghy sailing. After all – in a sailing dinghy you can do it sitting down.

Choosing a Dinghy

Before choosing a dinghy it is first necessary to decide on the kind of sailing that interests you most. If you simply wish to potter, don't pick a skittish and highly technical dinghy. If on the other hand you have decided to join the local club and sail with friends, pick whichever class of dinghy they sail. If top competition and plenty of travelling is what you want, you will need a boat with a strong and active class association and a good open meeting circuit.

Try to avoid buying a boat you fall in love with at first sight at a boat show, only to find that there is nowhere in your area you can race it.

Other Factors to Consider

Who will be sailing with you? A husband-and-wife team will probably not want a demanding, high-performance trapeze dinghy, but would find a fast 14 foot (4.27 m) boat good fun: an older couple might prefer the extra stability of, say, a Wayfarer, and so on.

How much maintenance are you prepared to do yourself? A wooden boat with varnished decks can look lovely, but it takes a great deal of time to maintain. A glassfibre boat may not turn so many heads, but will require less work.

Buying Second-hand

There are many ways to find the right second-hand dinghy: by asking (or advertising) at the local club; by looking at the 'for sale' cards in the local chandlers; or through the classified advertisements of a good dinghy sailing magazine.

There are distinct advantages in buying second-hand. With luck, you will be able to buy everything you need in a single purchase. With a new boat, many of the items you will need count as accessories and have to be bought separately. It is a great help if you can buy a road trailer and launching trolley together with the boat. But make sure they are the right kind. The wrong trailer can cause structural damage to your dinghy.

Ask a friend who knows about dinghies to come with you, or someone from the club or class you will join. Examine not only the hull, but the trailer, the sails, and the extra gear. When it comes to price, make sure that you are comparing like with like. Compare the ages of rival boats as well as their condition. Make sure that the trailer, launching trolley, sails and cover are included in the deal.

Look at sail numbers and compare these with the newest numbers in the class. Usually the lower the number, the older the boat, and therefore the lower the price.

In the same way that the best time to sell a boat is at the beginning of the season, the best time to buy one is at the end of it.

Ideally, you can try and have a trial sail in the sort of dinghy you think you might like, but this is not always possible. You might have become attached to a particular class at, say, a sailing school or an adventure holiday and thus want to stick with that, but most probably you will choose either the class that your friends sail, or the class that is sailed in your local club.

Dinghy Classes

The many varieties of class dinghy can be recognised by their differing sail insignia, normally carried on the mainsail along with the boat's individual class and sail number.

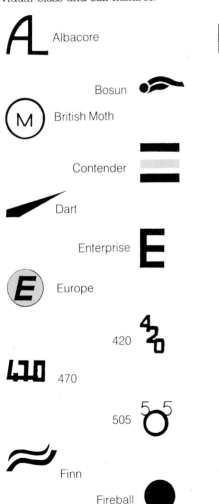

Albacore

Bosun

British Moth

Contender

Dart

Enterprise

Europe

420

470

505

Finn

Fireball

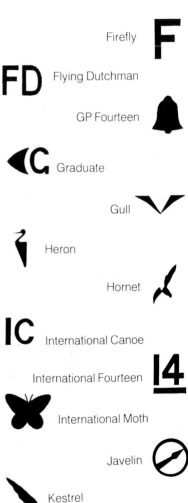

Firefly

Flying Dutchman

GP Fourteen

Graduate

Gull

Heron

Hornet

International Canoe

International Fourteen

International Moth

Javelin

Kestrel

Laser

Laser 2

Marauder

Merlin Rocket

Miracle

Mirror

National Eighteen

National Twelve

OK

Optimist

Osprey

Otter

Pacer

Phantom

Scorpion

Shearwater

Snipe

Solo

Spark

Tasar

Topper

Tornado

Unicorn

Wanderer

Wayfarer

Parts of a Dinghy

What distinguishes the sailing dinghy from other forms of sailing boat is the centreboard or centreplate. This acts as a form of drop keel and its primary function is to give the dinghy a grip on the water: the sails exert a sideways force on the dinghy which is resisted by the centreboard and the resultant force is what moves the dinghy forwards through the water. A dinghy carries no ballast and relies on the moveable weight of its crew to keep it upright.

The dinghy is steered by the rudder which is itself controlled by the tiller, the combined rudder and tiller unit being called the helm – hence the word 'helmsman' for the person who steers the dinghy.

The vertical spar which holds the sail aloft is the mast, the horizontal spar supporting the mainsail being the boom. The mast is supported (or 'stayed') by the standing rigging: the stay at the front being the forestay, those at the side being called shrouds. The two fore-and-aft sails are the jib (at the bow) and the mainsail, with the spinnaker being used only downwind. The ropes which control the sails are called sheets, those which take them aloft (haul them up) being called halyards. The three corners of the sail are the head, the tack and the clew.

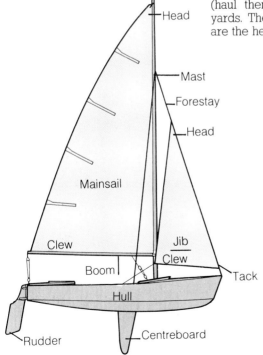

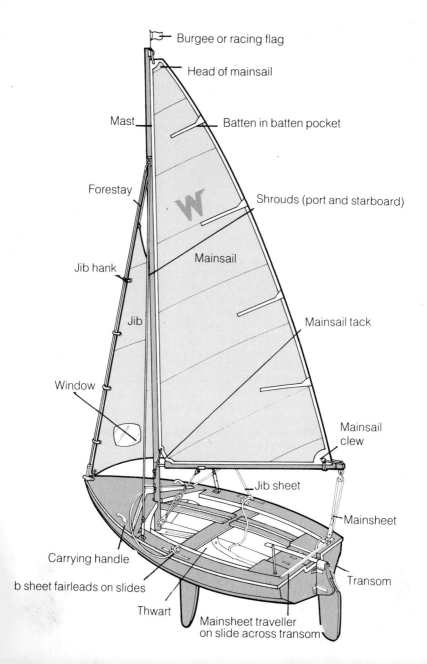

Burgee or racing flag

Head of mainsail

Mast

Batten in batten pocket

Forestay

Shrouds (port and starboard)

W

Mainsail

Jib hank

Jib

Mainsail tack

Window

Mainsail clew

Jib sheet

Mainsheet

Carrying handle

b sheet fairleads on slides

Transom

Thwart

Mainsheet traveller on slide across transom

The tack is the corner where the sail is attached to the boat or spar, while the clew is the leeward or aft corner. Jib and spinnaker sheets are attached to their respective clews and the spinnaker is further supported by its own boom, normally and simply called the spinnaker pole. The pole is controlled by the spinnaker guy.

Spars and Rigging

The spars of the dinghy are her mast and her boom, the last being the spar that supports and extends the foot of the mainsail. These are supported and controlled by the rigging – the coverall name given all the wires and ropes which are used to control the sails, the spars and in fact anything else.

Rigging which is not normally adjusted while sailing is known as standing rigging, while rigging which is or can be adjusted is called running rigging. In most dinghies the standing rigging consists of the forestay, which supports the mast from forward, at the bow, and the side stays which are called shrouds.

Standing Rigging

The standing rigging is set up when the mast is stepped and, once properly adjusted, is altered only if the rigging itself stretches or the rake or position of the mast is to be moved to alter the balance of the boat. In the simplest case, each leg of rigging is attached to the boat with lashings to each of the chainplates (the fittings which take the shrouds) and in the case of the forestay to the stemhead fitting or the stem plate.

This rather crude method of attachment is entirely adequate for a small dinghy used for pottering but on a bigger dinghy or where more sophisticated control is required, bottlescrews or rigging adjusters are used.

Running Rigging

Running rigging is any rigging which needs to be or can be adjusted while sailing. Most obvious are the lines used to control the sails: these are called *sheets*. Obviously, the mainsheet controls the mainsail and the jibsheets the jib. On a simple dinghy there may be little other running rigging. Such items as the mainsail outhaul may be only a simple lashing, but on a complicated racing dinghy there will be running rigging to control and adjust not merely the main outhaul but also the cunningham, the kicker, the centreboard, jibsheet barber haulers – virtually every control on the boat.

Rudder and Centreboard

The rudder and the centreboard are fundamental items of the dinghy's equipment.

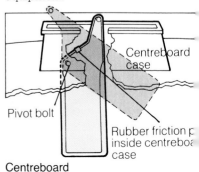

Centreboard case

Pivot bolt

Rubber friction p
inside centreboa
case

Centreboard

The rudder allows the dinghy to be steered: moving the rudder to one side or the other creates an imbalance of water pressure which forces the stern to move sideways. If the centreboard were not fitted (or is raised) the stern would just skid sideways and the dinghy would yaw more or less uncontrollably. However, if the centreboard is lowered

Rudder

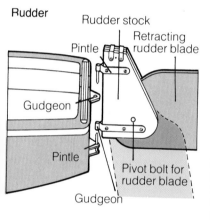

Rudder stock

Pintle

Retracting rudder blade

Gudgeon

Pintle

Pivot bolt for rudder blade

Gudgeon

even a small amount it acts as a pivot point on which the dinghy can turn smartly.

The rudder is turned by the tiller – the horizontal arm which protrudes from the rudder head into the boat. Most tillers are fitted with a 'tiller extension', a hinged arm designed to enable the helmsman to reach the tiller even when sitting out on the deck.

Some beginners have difficulty mastering the tiller extension – but if you think of it not as a 'tiller extension' but as your own 'arm extension'

there will be no problem.

The rudder is 'hung' on fittings on the transom to allow it to turn freely: these matched fittings are the pintles and gudgeons. The pintle is the pin-like spike; the gudgeon is the ring through which the pintle fits.

Rudder hangings should always be through-bolted to the transom: if you buy a secondhand dinghy and the rudder fittings are merely screwed on to the transom, remove them and bolt them on. If you do not, sooner or latter they will work loose.

Gooseneck

The mainboom attaches to the mast by means of a universal joint fitting called the gooseneck. This allows the boom to swing horizontally from side to side and also vertically. Goosenecks are either fixed or sliding, the former being simpler and often stronger but the latter being more useful as they provide a means of tensioning the luff (leading edge) of the sail.

The sliding gooseneck moves in a track, either fixed to the mast or formed by a widened-out section of

Tiller

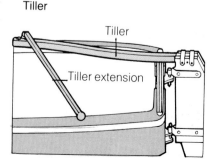

Tiller

Tiller extension

the luff groove for the sail. The vertical height of the slider – and thus the amount of tension in the luff of the mainsail – is set either by a spring-loaded plunger which locates in one of a series of holes in the track, or by a thumbscrew device which locks the gooseneck slider in the luff groove.

Kicking Straps

The kicking strap is used to limit the amount of vertical swing in the boom. If a kicking strap, sometimes simply called a kicker (or a vang in the USA), is not used, then as the mainsheet is eased the boom can swing up as well as out. This allows the sail to twist at the top. On a run this can even be dangerous since the head of the mainsail can be twisted off so much that it pushes on the leeward side of the mast, caus-

Goosenecks

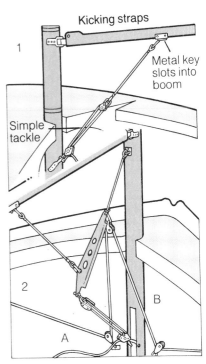

Above: Two types of kicker (sometimes called vang). On lever type (**2**) line A gives coarse control, line B gives fine adjustment.

ing excessive rolling or maybe a capsize. The simplest form of kicker is a multi-part block and tackle, but a carefully rigged lever can also be used. In fine sail trim, the kicker is used to set the required amount of tension in the mainsail leech.

Rigging Adjusters

A rigging adjuster – sometimes called a shroud adjuster or shroud plate – is simply two matched metal strips, usually stainless steel, each with a series of corresponding holes

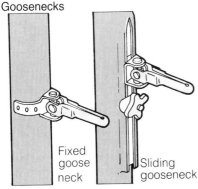

Above: Fixed and sliding gooseneck fittings – the sliding type can be used to adjust luff tension. With both types the main halyard should be secured before the boom is put on the gooseneck.

along its length. One end of the pair of strips is attached to the chainplate using a clevis pin. The hard eye of the shroud end is held between the strips with another clevis pin pushed into one of the pairs of holes. The tension in the shroud can be varied by moving the pin to a higher or lower pair of holes.

If shroud plates are used, a bottle-screw must be used on the lower end of the forestay. This consists of a cylindrical barrel which is threaded internally and into the ends of which fit two threaded rods, each with a Y-fitting on the end.

The end of the forestay fits into one Y-fitting, the other Y-fitting is attached to the stemplate. Turning the barrel, or bottle, of the screw increases or decreases the overall length of the combined fitting, allowing the tension in the forestay to be adjusted.

Blocks

A block is what the ironmonger and the scoutmaster call a pulley. It is used to lead a line wherever it is wanted, or in conjunction with other blocks to give a mechanical purchase: for example in the kicker and the mainsheet.

The simple block may have a swivel incorporated in its mounting to enable it to turn on its own axis.

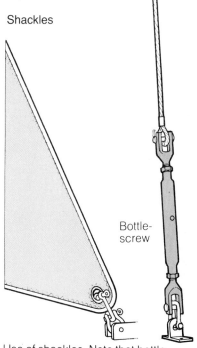

Shackles

Bottle-screw

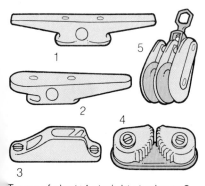

Types of cleat: **1** straight staghorn; **2** simple jamming cleat – the line is led round the round end of the cleat and jammed under the vee-end; **3** and **4** are patent jamming cleats; **5** is double-sheave block with swivel.

Use of shackles. Note that bottle-screw is attached to deck plate by shackle to permit universal movement: attaching direct could limit movement and cause screw to bend.

Bends and Hitches

Whole books have been written about bends and hitches, but for the dinghy sailor half-a-dozen well-known knots are sufficient. Learn to tie them automatically and even practice doing them one-handed. Modern synthetic ropes have much less friction than the natural fibre ropes in use when most knots were developed.

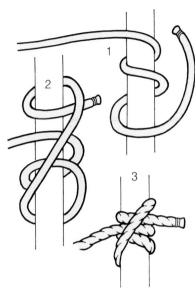

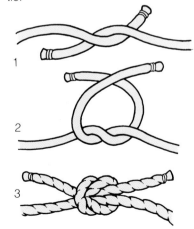

Rolling hitch
Non-slip version of clove hitch: the extra turn locks-up the hitch, prevents it pulling along. Useful rope-on-rope tie.

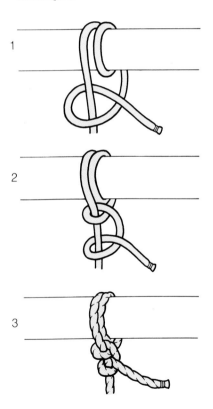

Round turn and two half hitches
Provides greater security than the clove hitch offers.

Reef knot
Rarely used. If you must use it, leave one end tucked in as a half-bow.

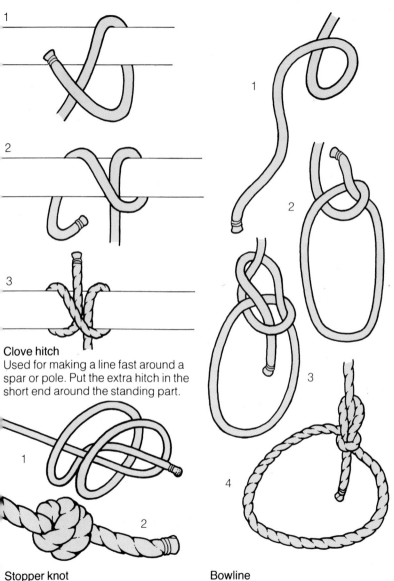

Clove hitch

Used for making a line fast around a spar or pole. Put the extra hitch in the short end around the standing part.

Stopper knot

Use for ends of sheets, control lines etc. Far superior to figure-of-eight knot as this one will not jam-up solid.

Bowline

Use it for all sorts of jobs. Practise tying it in different positions and even with one hand.

Rigging the Jib

Take the jib out of the bag and unroll the sail, following down the luff from head to tack to make sure there are no twists in the sail.

Attach the tack to the bow fitting, making sure that the hard eye – called a thimble – in the tack will be lined up fore and aft when the sail is hoisted.

Next, hank-on the luff to the fore-stay. Two types of hank are in common use: the older fashioned and heavier piston hank and the more recently developed snap hank. On a piston hank, pulling back the plunger allows the hank to be hooked around the forestay; releasing it lets the pin go forward to close the hank. On most sails, all the hanks will be lashed to the sail the same way, usually with the piston on the starboard side of the sail. Snap hanks, of moulded nylon, consist of two half-hooks set one above the other, with the hooks working in opposing directions. The hank is slipped on to the forestay on its side then turned through 90° to engage the hooks. Make sure you put all the hanks on the same way, otherwise the luff of the sail will be twisted.

Before attaching the halyard, check aloft to make sure the lead is clear and the halyard has not got a turn around the forestay. Halyards either shackle on to a hard eye on the head of the jib or, if the halyard is rope, are tied to the sail. The correct term (tying is something you do to parcels) is 'bent on' – hence the term *bend*, meaning a certain type of knot. The bend to use is either the round turn and two half-hitches (see page 22) or the sheet bend (rope out through the eye, round the back to the front again and tucked under itself).

Next attach the sheets. These might be made up with an eye and a shackle, or might be one long line. If the second, take the rope, middle it so you have two ends the same length and pass one end through the clew-eye. Bring the end back and form a half-hitch, tied through the clew-eye and keeping the two ends the same length. Reeve the sheets through the fairleads: on most but not all dinghies the sheets lead outside the shrouds.

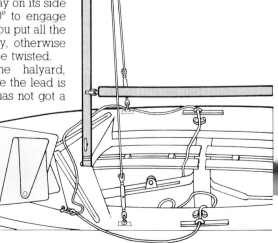

Now hoist the sail and be prepared for it to flog wildly if the wind is of any strength.

If a halyard hook is fitted, hook the long eye in the wire halyard over the hook and then set the lever in whichever notch will give maximum luff tension (while still allowing you to pull the lever up over-centre and lock it).

If the halyard is made up on a cleat, make it up as described for the main halyard.

Making up a halyard on a cleat, there is no need to wrap the rope round and round the cleat: indeed too many turns will increase the chance of the halyard slipping. Take one full turn over the cleat and follow with a figure-of-eight. Then take one more turn and jam the loop of this turn under the loop of the figure-of-eight. Finish off by coiling the halyard, pulling a bight through, giving it half-a-twist and looping it over the top of the cleat.

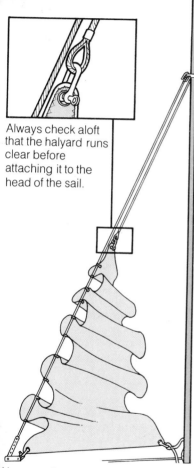

Always check aloft that the halyard runs clear before attaching it to the head of the sail.

Above and opposite: The jib is made ready for hoisting ashore. First shackle the tack to the stem fitting. Then attach the sheets, or if they are kept attached to the sail reeve them outside the shrouds and through the fairleads. Hank the luff to the forestay and hoist.

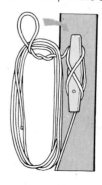

Rigging and Hoisting the Mainsail

If you establish a set pattern of working when putting the sails on, the job will become second nature to you and take half the time it otherwise might have done. First, run the foot on to the boom, sliding the bolt rope along the groove in the boom. Then secure the tack. Usually this is simply done with a clevis pin through the two lugs at the gooseneck end of the boom and through the tack eye of the sail.

Next rig, but do not tension, the clew outhaul. On a cruising or day-sailing dinghy this may be simply a lanyard from the end of the boom, through the clew eye of the sail and back to the boom end, maybe led several times to give a purchase. On a serious racing dinghy, the outhaul tension will be adjustable from inside the boat and while sailing.

Now fit the battens. If you fit them before you put the sail on the boom there is a greater risk of their being broken, so always put the sail on to the boom first. There are two types of batten and batten pocket: tie-in and push-in. Push-in batten pockets are closed at their outboard end, the batten sliding into the pocket through a slot on the top. The inner end of the batten locates against an elasticated stop at the front end of the pocket. The outboard end fits into the envelope formed by the pocket.

A tie-in batten has two holes through its outer end, with two light lanyards stitched to the outer end of the pocket. These go through the holes and are joined by a reef knot.

If the battens are tapered, the thinner end goes forward. Fit the bottom batten first, so that the sail

lies neatly in the boat, with the top batten uppermost, ready to attach the halyard.

The Main Halyard

Most main halyards shackle to the headboard of the mainsail. If you have just bought a dinghy and find it has an all-rope halyard, change it for

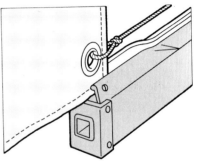

Above: Always put the sail on to the boom before inserting the battens. This lessens the chance of them being broken.

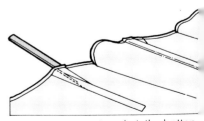

Above: In a patent pocket, the batten is slid in through a slot in the top of the pocket to locate against an elastic stop. The aft end of the batten is pushed into the pocket and held secure by the elastic.

wire-and-rope halyard if class rules permit. Even so-called "pre-stretched" rope stretches a bit under the sort of loads imposed by the mainsail luff under tension, and this makes good sail setting virtually impossible.

Hoisting the Sail

When ready to hoist, turn the dinghy so she sits head to wind. If the boom

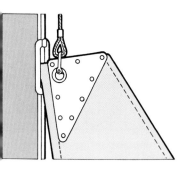

feed the luff of the mainsail into the mast groove (above) and hoist. Finally, push the boom on to the gooseneck (below). If a fixed gooseneck is used, pull the sail against the stretch of the luff rope.

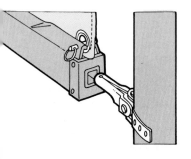

can be securely fixed on to the gooseneck, do it now but on many dinghies it is the kicker tension which keeps the boom on the gooseneck so the boom for the moment must be left lying in the boat. Make sure the mainsheet is clear to run and has plenty of slack, likewise make sure there is plenty of slack in the kicker or that it is not attached at this stage to the boom.

Hoist the sail and fit the boom on to the gooseneck, making up the halyard as described below. Fit the kicker and put a fair bit of tension on: this will stop the boom swinging wildly about but allow it to swing slowly. Make sure the mainsheet is slack, lest the sail fill and capsize the boat before you even get her afloat.

Tension the outhaul: if the outhaul is not adjustable while sailing, put sufficient tension in it to take the wrinkles out of the foot of the sail but not so much that a hard line appears along the foot of the sail, parallel to the boom.

Making up the Halyard

After hoisting, make up the halyard on the cleat as shown. Take one full turn over the cleat, form a figure-of-eight, and then do another turn. The second turn should jam under the turn of the figure-of-eight, using the rope's own friction for security. Adding extra turns merely bunches-up the cleat and increases the chances of the halyard slipping.

It is very dangerous to finish off with a half-hitch: the chances are it will jam solid at the worst possible moment and you will be unable to lower the sail.

Going Afloat

Now you are ready to go afloat. Check that you have everything in the boat that you will need: paddles, bailer (tied in) and so on. Check that the transom bungs are in and that the self-bailer (if there is one) is raised.

If the rudder is of the lifting blade variety, it can be put on now, the tiller fitted and the blade secured in the up position. Make sure that there are no lines, in particular the main-sheet or jib sheets, dangling over the deck edges ready to become caught up with the wheels of the launching trolley. Make sure, too, that you have a painter secured to the deck cleat or stemhead fitting so you can hold the boat while getting the launching trolley out of the way.

Launching off a Weather Shore
This is pretty easy. Traditionally boats are launched stern first (the stern has more buoyancy than the bow) so going afloat with the wind blowing off land means that the boat can be wheeled into the water while remaining head to wind.

Once the boat has floated off her trolley, one person holds her head to wind while the other disposes of the trolley above the high tide mark!

Next, one person gets aboard and lowers or partially lowers the rudder blade and centreboard to give some steerage. Person Two clambers on board, giving the bow a shove away from the shore at the same time. You can help the boat turn away from the wind by *backing* the jib – that is, pulling in the sheet on the weather side to sheet the sail to windward. It fills from the 'wrong' side (it backs)

and the bow will pay off away from the wind. If the boat starts going backwards, remember that the rudder and tiller work the wrong way – exactly like reversing a car.

Launching off a Lee Shore
This is more tricky. As you try to launch stern first, the wind is blow

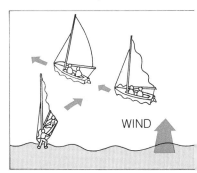

Above: Remember that the helm is reversed when going backwards. To turn the bow to starboard the tiller should be put over to starboard.

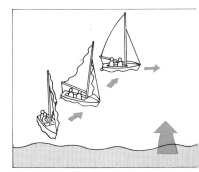

Launching off a Weather Shore
Keeping the centreboard up will allow the boat to blow sideways off the beach until deep water is reached. A lee shore is more tricky.

ng over the stern of the boat and hus into the mainsail. It will be necessary to hold the boat on her rolley to prevent her capsizing; as soon as she is afloat, the crew must wade into the water holding the bow o turn the dinghy head to wind. Only a little centreboard can be used until the dinghy is in deep water and it may be necessary to sail for a few yards with little or no rudder until the dinghy is in deeper water. Helmsman and crew have to work very much together: the helmsman looks after keeping the boat upright and moving, until everything is settled just keep the boat 'jogging along' while the crew does the tidying up. If the boat has a fixed rudder blade, it may be necessary either to paddle her off into water deep enough to put the rudder down, or to sail her using a paddle as a temporary steering oar.

Usually, you will have the jib sheeted but not fully home to give the sail plenty of drive, and will be using only about half the mainsail.

In some strong wind conditions it may be prudent not to hoist the sails until the dinghy is afloat. In these circumstances, one person will have to stand in the water holding the dinghy head to wind, while the other goes through the hoisting routine.

There is no hard and fast rule about how you get aboard, but usually the crew will hold the boat while the helmsman clambers in and sorts out the tangle of slack sheets and flapping sails, pulls down a little centreboard and puts down some rudder blade.

Then the crew wades the boat out as far as he can, turns her head away from the wind to let the sails begin to fill and scrambles aboard.

If it is blowing too hard to launch the dinghy with the mainsail hoisted, she can be launched with the jib up and flapping and the main bent on to the boom and ready to hoist. You can either hoist the mainsail while the crew is holding the boat head to wind in the water, or sail off under jib only.

Launching off a Lee Shore
Wade the boat out to where there is enough water to put some board down.

You can beat with about half board. The crew holds the bow head to wind while the helmsman clambers aboard.

Points of Sailing

STARBOARD TACK

Close hauled

Close fetch

Beam reach

Broad reach

STARBOARD GYBE

A sailing dinghy is propelled forwards by the wind blowing across the sails. If the dinghy is held head to wind, the wind blows evenly along both sides of the sail, which merely acts as a flag. As the bow is turned off the wind, so the wind blows more into one side than the other until the sail takes up its natural curve.

For all practical purposes, this does not happen until the dinghy's bows are turned off the wind at an angle of about 45°. It is the air flowing along the sail, both on the windward and the leeward side, that causes the sail to drive the boat along.

With the sails sheeted in as close as they will naturally go, but still taking up their proper shape, the dinghy is *close hauled*.

As the bows are turned further away from the direction in which the wind is blowing (*bearing away*), the sheets have to be eased. This process keeps the front part of the sails at such an angle to the wind that the airflow striking the sail divides evenly on both sides.

When the dinghy is sailing at right angles to the direction of the wind, she is *reaching*, or sailing on a reach. As it bears away further, the reach becomes broader until eventually the boat is pointing in the direction in which the wind is blowing. Now she is *running*, or sailing with the wind.

If we continue the turn, the wind will start to blow into the mainsail from the wrong side. We anticipate this by bringing the sails across to the other side. This is called *gybing*.

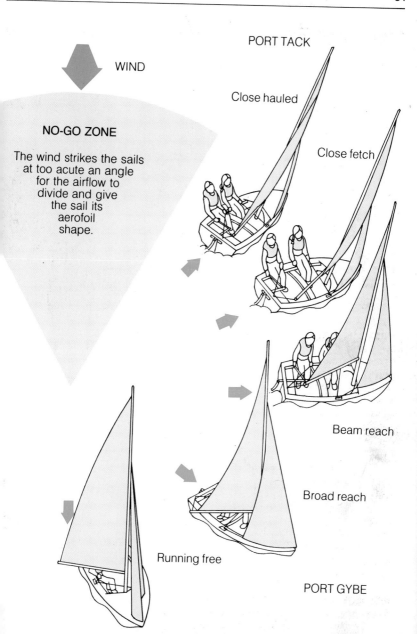

WIND

PORT TACK

Close hauled

Close fetch

NO-GO ZONE

The wind strikes the sails
at too acute an angle
for the airflow to
divide and give
the sail its
aerofoil
shape.

Beam reach

Broad reach

Running free

PORT GYBE

Tacking

WIND

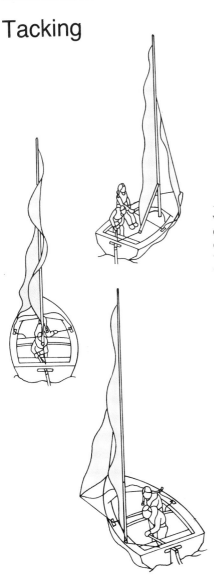

way and then the other. This procedure is called *tacking* and, just to be confusing, the word describes both the whole zig-zagging process and the actual action of turning the boat through the wind direction (the eye of the wind). With the wind blowing across the port side of the dinghy, we are on *port tack*. With the wind on the starboard side we are on *starboard tack*.

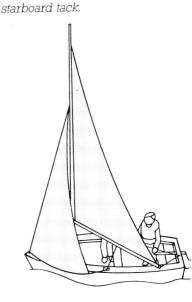

We can only sail close hauled at about 45° to the wind. To reach a destination within the two 45° angles, we must zig-zag, first one

Gybing

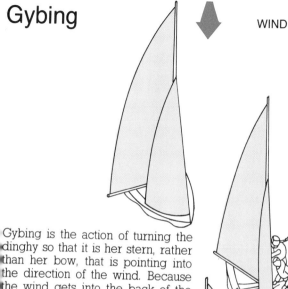

WIND

Gybing is the action of turning the dinghy so that it is her stern, rather than her bow, that is pointing into the direction of the wind. Because the wind gets into the back of the sails, the mainsail especially, quite abruptly the suddenness of the gybe

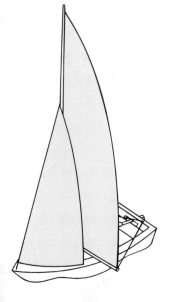

can be alarming. Good co-ordination, however, takes the sting out of gybing. As the boat bears away the crew balances the boat while the helmsman catches the mainsheet by all its parts and pulls it across, steering the boat in a firm but gentle arc.

Changing Course

Crew move inboard

We have seen how the sails have be trimmed to suit the dinghy course in relation to wind direction Next, we need to look at the way which the boat itself is trimmed, balanced.

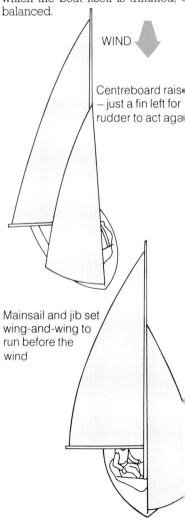

WIND

Centreboard rais — just a fin left for rudder to act aga

Mainsail and jib set wing-and-wing to run before the wind

As the sheets are eased, the heeling forces on the dinghy become less and the crew can move inboard. As the boat begins to sail with the wind rather than against it, the centreboard will be needed less and so can be raised. Some board, however, will still be needed to give the rudder something to act against and to provide a pivot upon which the boat can turn, thus keeping her easy to steer.

Eventually, the jib will be blanketed by the main sail, and with the dinghy almost running free the jib can be set on the opposite side to the main, or wing-and-wing. Although the strength of the breeze should keep the jib filled, life is made easier and the jib can be spread out better by using a jib-stick or whisker pole to boom it out. Running straight downwind, the crew sit on either side to keep the boat balanced.

Turning towards the wind (called *hardening-up*) we trim the boat differently. First, crew weight should be moved forward to stop the stern from dragging. As the sails are sheeted home and we try to sail towards the wind, the heeling force of the wind in the sails becomes greater, so it is necessary to sit out and use the crew as a counter-weight. The wind will also try to blow the boat sideways: the result is called leeway, and the centreboard is used to minimize the amount of leeway the dinghy makes.

Sailing close hauled, the board should be right down to present the maximum amount of sideways (later-

WIND

Crew weight outboard as the dinghy comes on the wind. Keep the weight central fore-and-aft.

al) area, and thus resist the force that is trying to push the dinghy side-ways. This resistance put up by the centreboard, acting underneath the dinghy as the sails act above, further increases the heeling movement so more strenuous efforts are needed to keep the boat upright.

Returning to Shore

With the breeze blowing off the land, returning to shore is relatively easy because as we beat in to the shore we can slow the boat by luffing up (sailing almost directly head to wind). With the breeze onshore, it is best to lower the mainsail a little way offshore and blow in under jib. Close to the shore, the jib can be let fly completely to slow the dinghy down.

Rudder blade and centreboard must be lifted before they hit the bottom, and one crew-member has to go over the side to catch and stop the dinghy. It may be necessary to hold her head to wind and clear of the beach while the trolley is re-covered and this can mean standing almost chest deep in the water,

especially if there is any surf. Wave breaking over the dinghy may f her up with sand and water, ar there is a risk of damage by pound ing, particularly on a shingle beac.

Putting the boat on to her trolley such conditions requires speed ar co-ordination. Get the dinghy cle of the water as quickly as possible minimise the risk of damage.

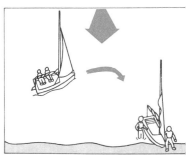

Above: Coming ashore with an onshore breeze, you can either drop the mainsail and come in under jib, c drop both sails and blow ashore.

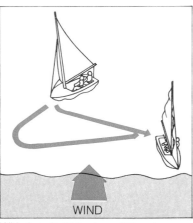

With the wind blowing off the shore, slow the boat by luffing up and nudge gently into the shore, raising the centreboard and rudder. The crew hops into the water to help the boat ashore.

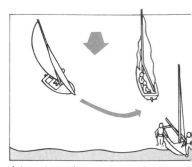

If there is surf, you must quickly get the dinghy up the beach before she filled with sand, or worse, damaged by pounding.

Care of Sails

ils are expensive items, and they
e the dinghy's only source of
ower so it pays to look after them
roperly. Yet when the day's sailing
done, it is amazing to see how
arelessly some people treat them.

Never bundle sails into a bag.
ich crumpling breaks down the
sins and fillers used in the manu-
cture of the sailcloth and not only
akes the cloth less efficient itself
it also causes the sails to lose their
ape very quickly.

Before sails are put in the bag
ey should ideally be washed off
id dried. This is not always poss-
le but if facilities permit, hose the
ils off with water and then spread

them out to dry. Never, ever, dry
sails by hoisting them loosely and
allowing them to flap and flog in the
breeze like washing.

Fold sails by flaking them in even
folds parallel with the foot. The job is
not difficult with two people.

Folding the Mainsail

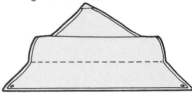

1 Fold the sail concertina fashion. The
first fold must be deep if the sail has a
window (don't crease the plastic).

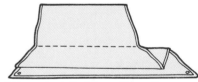

2 Keep the luff of the sail together,
allowing the leech to work its way
naturally towards the luff.

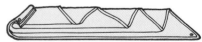

3 The size of the folds is dictated by
the size of the sail bag, but keep them
as big and loose as possible.

4 Stow the battens (which should
already have been removed) and the
racing flag inside the rolled sail.

elow: Ideally the jib should be folded
the same way as the mainsail, but a
 with a stiff wire luffrope can be
lled as shown.

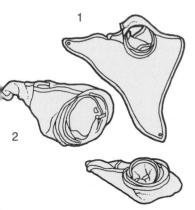

the jib sheets stay on the sail, try
id dry them before putting them
vay with the sail in the sailbag.

Learning to Sail

There are many different ways to learn about dinghy sailing. One way is simply to start sailing with a friend, perhaps just pottering around. The difficulty is that what is learned, and how quickly, depends on how good the friend is, how often he or she takes you sailing and what sort of sailing he does.

Alternatively, you might go along to the local club and find someone prepared to take on a novice as crew. The snag with that is that you might well wind up with the wrong sort of teacher: good helmsmen usually prefer, and can usually get, experienced crews so the novice is left only with a bad or inexperienced helmsman. The novice not only learns slowly but in the process picks up a good deal of nonsense, wrong information and probably a few bad habits as well.

Sailing Schools

A better way for the complete stranger to learn the rudiments of dinghy sailing is to go to a reputable sailing school. Any good school should be able to teach the simple basics within a five-day residential course and many national authorities have their own training and teaching schemes with a syllabus that commercial schools can follow.

The National Dinghy Sailing Scheme

One of the best schemes in the world is run by Britain's Royal Yachting Association, and it is so good that parts of it have been copied by other countries.

Called the National Dinghy Sailing Scheme it has been adopted by commercial sailing schools, local authorities, sea training organizations and education committees for use in schools. It contains a complete and standardized syllabus going from basic sailing right up to advanced racing techniques, as well as including courses for those who want to become instructors and coaches themselves.

The basis of the scheme is the RYA National Dinghy Sailing Certificate to which can be added Seamanship and Racing endorsements. The basic course covers general safety and basic dinghy handling in light winds. All the aspects of dinghy handling already touched on in this book are covered in detail: rowing and paddling, handling boats ashore, rigging, launching and recovery, capsize and man overboard drills as well as general sailing practice.

The further courses, which are designed to be attended about once a year, with the dinghy sailor gaining experience in his own boat or at his own club in the meantime, cover racing both in basic form and in advanced detail and, for those who want to try some further afield sailing, navigation and general seamanship.

Details of the scheme and a list of sailing schools in Britain which are approved to operate the scheme are available from the Royal Yachting Association.

Right: Over 200 sailing schools, sailing clubs and teaching establishments operate the RYA tuition scheme.

Man Overboard

If one crew member falls overboard, the safest technique is immediately to turn the boat on to a beam reach (1). Ease the mainsail to slow the boat down, and when you have collected your wits, tack the boat and turn back (2). Go on to a broad reach, and sail to a position (3) downwind of the person in the water, so that you can luff slowly towards him with the sheets eased. On the final approach, let the jib go and use the mainsail to control the speed of the boat. The person in the water, having first grabbed the shroud, or a rope trailed over the side, should work to the stern of the dinghy, where the person on board can most easily help.

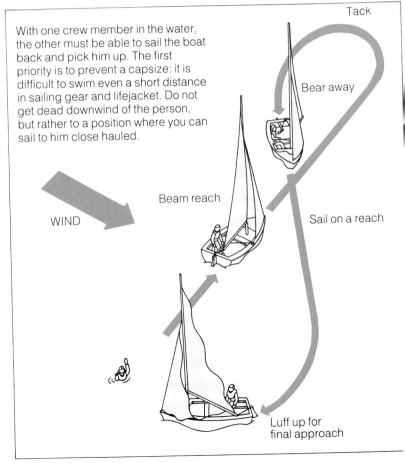

With one crew member in the water, the other must be able to sail the boat back and pick him up. The first priority is to prevent a capsize: it is difficult to swim even a short distance in sailing gear and lifejacket. Do not get dead downwind of the person, but rather to a position where you can sail to him close hauled.

Tack

Bear away

WIND

Beam reach

Sail on a reach

Luff up for final approach

Capsizing and Righting

a modern dinghy with built-in buoyancy or with buoyancy bags stalled, and with crew wearing good chill-proof clothing and buoyancy aids, capsizing need not be a disaster. Indeed in a racing dinghy capsizing might be commonplace and the ability to right quickly and be away again is an important part of the racer's sailing repertoire.

Sooner or later a capsize occurs: the good dinghy sailor should need no help in righting his boat and covering the situation completely. In theory, a capsized dinghy lies on her side with the sails pointing more or less downwind. It is righted by having one or both the crew stand on the centreboard and using crew weight to cantilever the boat upright, the crew climbing back into the boat as she comes upright.

On a big dinghy which has been overwhelmed, this is just how it sometimes happens, but in other cases things are not so straightforward. On smaller dinghies there will not be room for both crew members on the board and in any case one or both may have gone into the water during the capsize. If this happens, get into a situation with one of you on each side of the capsized hull. One person then climbs up on to the high side, either up over the centreboard case and deck while the other hangs on to the board, preventing the dinghy inverting, or by clambering on to the board while the person on the other side stays swimming in the cockpit.

On a first capsize, it will not normally be necessary to lower the sails, but if it is blowing very hard; if

this is yet another capsize of many; if you are tired and have been trying to get the boat up for some time, only to have her blow over on you again and again, then take the sails off with the boat on her side, pulling them down the mast into the cockpit. This is where you are very glad you did not use a half-hitch on the main halyard cleat (see page 27).

With one person on the board, use a jib sheet flung over the high side to help you hang out and bring the boat up. Do not go too far down the board lest it should break: stay near the root of the board at its strongest, widest part. If the dinghy

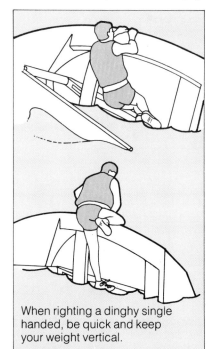

When righting a dinghy single handed, be quick and keep your weight vertical.

capsized on a reach, the person on the cockpit side may have to push the board through before you can start to right the boat.

As the dinghy comes up, the person on the other side either stays in the water by the shrouds or tries to stay in the boat. Either way the idea is to have a person each side of the upright, semi-waterlogged dinghy to prevent her blowing over again. From this position, each can take turns balancing the boat as the other climbs aboard.

The Scoop Method

Using the so-called 'scoop method' allows the person on the cockpit side to lie alongside the plate case as the boat begins to right herself. They are then literally scooped into the boat as she comes upright. A really slick pair, righting a dinghy with built-in buoyancy such as the 505 or 470, can practice so that the one on the board hops over the weather side as the dinghy rights, leaving them both in the boat and ready to sail on. If the one on the

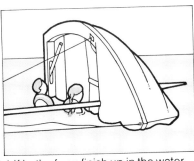

1 If both of you finish up in the water on the cockpit side, one swims round the stern to the centreboard . . .

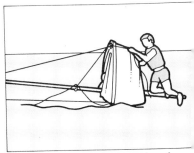

2 . . . climbs up on the board and grabs a jib sheet. The other stays close to the centreboard case .

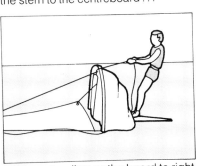

3 When standing on the board to right the dinghy, stay close to the keel to lessen the risk of breaking the board.

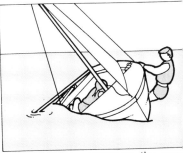

4 As the dinghy comes up, the one the water is scooped aboard and ca then help the other back in.

ɔard is not quite quick enough the
ʌe scooped into the boat can bal-
ʌce the boat while the other climbs
ɔoard over the side at the shroud.

Once upright, it is usually best to
llow the dinghy to lie beam on to
ɛ wind, with the sails eased right
f and the centreboard raised to
llow her to blow sideways while
ɔu sort out the mess.

ʒhting an Inverted Dinghy

the dinghy inverts completely,
ɔth crew members must start at the

same side to right her. One or both
climb on the gunwale to bring her to
a normal capsized condition, choosing the side which will leave the
dinghy lying with the rig downwind.
There is then a choice. You can
either pause while one sailor swims
round the other side or proceed to
right the dinghy with one person
holding on to the lower gunwale. As
the dinghy comes upright that
person is swept down and under the
boat to emerge on the other side of
the righted dinghy.

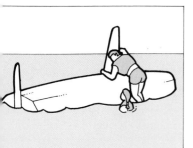

If the dinghy inverts, you may both
ɛ needed to bring her into a position
ɔm which she can be righted.

2 Stand first on the gunwale. If she
won't come up, use a jib sheet to let you
hang out and exert more leverage.

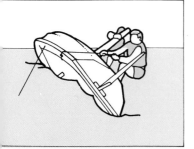

As she comes up, one of you prepares
drop back into the water while the
her climbs up on to the centreboard.

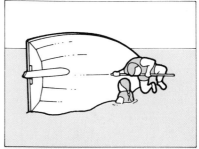

4 From here the person in the water
goes round the other side by
swimming round the stern .

Safety Equipment

It is asking for trouble not be safety conscious when dinghy sailing. When racing and sailing in a club environment there is usually a minimum amount of safety and emergency equipment which must be carried to comply with club or class rules: when sailing alone, adequate safety, or more correctly self-help, equipment is even more important.

Virtually all safety-conscious books and organizations tell you to wear a lifejacket at all times. That is easy to say and no doubt good advice, but there are occasions when there is no joy like sailing a dinghy on a sunny day in a sparkling

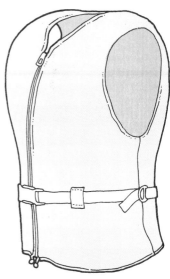

Above: A neat buoyancy waistcoat is adequate for most types of dinghy sailing and does not impede movem

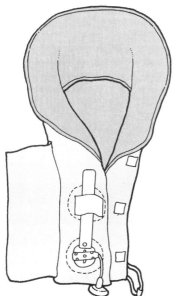

A self-inflating lifejacket with gas bottle and manual operating toggle. The flap closes over bottle and toggle.

A mouth-inflating lifejacket. Note whistle and lifting strap: doubtless very safe but a bit on the bulky side

breeze with only a pair of shorts or a swimming costume on. This book's advice is therefore: have a very good reason for not wearing at least a buoyancy aid.

The trouble with most institution-approved lifejackets (British Standards Institute, US Coast Guard, etc) is that to pass the stringent requirements they have to be made more buoyant, hence more bulky, than is good for dinghy sailing. Indeed some lifejackets are so bulky they virtually ensure you will need help and rescue, since you will be unable to clamber aboard your capsized

Good, non-slip shoes with soft soles prevent toes from being stubbed and feet cut on beaches, while dinghy boots with reinforced ankles are useful for hooking feet under toestraps.

Useful items of equipment
1 Dinghy shoe. 2 Dinghy boot. 3 Plastic bucket for bailing, with sponge. 4 A good long warp. 5 A canvas bag can be useful. 6 Paddle, which should be kept well secured. 7 Folding grapnel.

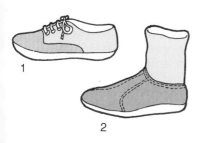

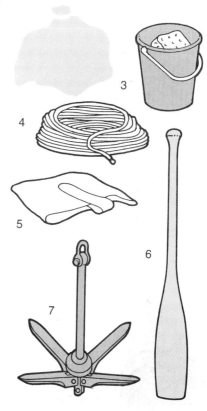

dinghy unaided. A slim-fitting buoyancy aid can be more all-round use than a bulky and cumbersome lifejacket.

Ensure you carry a bucket and/or a shaped bailer, secured in the dinghy with a lanyard long enough to allow it to be used without being untied. At least one paddle, again carried in retaining clips or otherwise secured, and for anything other than escorted racing, an anchor of at least the folding type. These grapnels, however, do not make good anchors for general use.

Clothing

In recent years, dinghy-sailing clothes have received almost as much attention as ski-wear, and fashionable sailing suits and specialized garments are widely available.

The requirements of the racing sailor, afloat for only an hour or two, are different from those of the day sailor or cruising dinghy enthusiast who will want to stay warm, dry and comfortable for long periods afloat. For the racer, the avoidance of wind chill is more important than staying dry. The racer has a wide choice of clothing systems to adopt.

Wetsuit
The sailor's wetsuit was developed from the scuba diver's suit: made from neoprene, it is designed to let in but retain water, which then becomes heated by body warmth and acts as an insulating layer. Older wetsuits had the disadvantage of not being at all waterproof: this could mean too much water coming through the suit or draining out, so that the water next to the wearer's body was constantly changing and thus never becoming properly heated. This caused excessive heat loss. Wearing a wind and waterproof overall over the wetsuit counteracts this problem to a great extent, while newer designs of wetsuit (called 'steamers' in the gimmick-ridden world of windsurfing) use a waterproof outer layer to achieve the same effect. There was a time, too, when all wetsuits, like all Henry Ford cars, were black, but modern materials enable fashion-conscious sailors to choose their wetsuit in a variety of colours.

A wetsuit, however, is an expensive one-piece garment made from soft and poorly wearing material. It is sensible therefore to wear over it either waterproof trousers and smock or a one-piece, lightweight nylon overall.

Drysuit
The drysuit is a lightweight version of the sealed suit worn by deepsea and clearance divers. Made from waterproof material, it is sealed by

The standard dinghy sailing outfit of woolly hat, smock and trousers and dinghy boots.

tight-fitting, lightweight rubber grommets at neck and cuffs, and has either rubber feet or further seals at the ankles. Drysuits tend to be more cumbersome than wetsuits and are even more vulnerable to friction damage, so again are usually worn under a dinghy suit.

Overalls

Good waterproof overalls are essential for the daysailer who probably does not want the bother of either a drysuit or wetsuit. These can be of the one-piece type or might comprise either smock and trousers or front-opening jacket and trousers. One problem with waist-high, self-supporting trousers is that the constant movement in a seated position can gradually pull down the trousers – usually just at the moment a wave

goes up the back of your smock. Chest-high trousers with shoulder straps overcome both these difficulties.

Gloves

Gloves are worn primarily to prevent chafe and rope-blisters, rather than for warmth. Good dinghy gloves have a reinforced palm and leave the fingertips and thumb open, for undoing shackles and similar jobs. This sort of glove can be worse than useless in cold weather, since it is not waterproof.

Hats

Even for those with a thick head of hair, heat loss through the head can be considerable: in cold weather a warm hat, usually of wool, is strongly recommended.

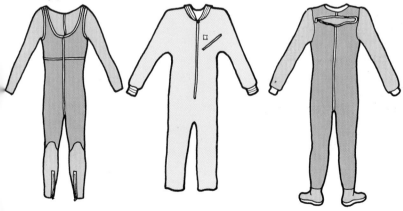

Wetsuits are now available in a galaxy of styles and a spectrum of colours. Zips at ankles facilitate getting suit on and off.

Many dinghy sailors wear a protective one-piece lightweight overall to guard against wear and tear to expensive wetsuits.

A drysuit with rubber seals at neck and wrists. It may have either seals at ankles or lightweight rubber feet. Great for winter sailing.

Part 2
Dinghy Racing
Organization

The Class System

Racing dinghies are organized in classes, each class being a particular type or design of dinghy. There are two types of dinghy class, one-design classes and restricted design classes. In a one-design class all the dinghies are supposed to be as nearly as possible the same: they are all built to the same design, often of the same material. As well as having the same shaped hull, the same class rules strictly define the dimensions of the rig, and so on.

Within the one-design concept, some classes are more strict than others: a very strict one-design class is the Laser, where hulls, spars, sails, and even fittings have to be identical and usually purchased from the same supplier. Some one-design classes, such as the 505 or the Hornet, insist on strict one-design hulls but permit a measure of freedom in deck layout.

Restricted Class

In a Restricted class, certain design parameters are defined, such as overall length, sail area, and minimum weight, but within those limits designers are free to draw and build a dinghy which incorporates their own ideas: the best-known example of a Restricted Design dinghy is probably the International Fourteen.

Class Organization

Within the overall class system there are three categories of class organization: International, National and local. International classes are those whose affairs are administered

through the International Yacht Racing Union (IYRU). They are normally world-wide classes and are raced in many countries: they hold world and European championship and all the classes raced in th Olympics are International.

The 505, a thoroughbred racing dinghy: easy to sail adequately, but very demanding to sail really well.

National and Local Classes

In Britain, National classes have their affairs administered through the Royal Yachting Association and local classes have their affairs administered by their own class association. There is, however, considerable overlap in terms of size and distribution of the class: a class such as the International Contender is numerically quite small, while the GP14, neither officially National nor International, has over 100,000 boats and is raced all round the world.

Races

Dinghy races are organized on many levels. The most common of these are local races, organized by and for members of a particular club and open only to them; open events, organized by a class association and open to any boat in the class; and championships. The championship of the class might be just a bigger-than-average open meeting or it may be a qualifiers-only event, depending on the size and competitive level of the class.

Rules

Dinghy races are held under a strict set of rules called the International Yacht Racing Rules, usually known as 'the racing rules'. These are established by the IYRU and are revised, usually only slightly, every four years, the revision taking place immediately after each Olympic Games.

The racing rules apply to all races run by official (or affiliated, as they are properly termed) yacht and sailing clubs. In addition, each race has its own set of sailing instructions which set out the time of the start, the course to be sailed and any special regulations that might apply.

The particular rules of the class also apply for each race within that class: for example, some classes do not permit the use of spinnakers while racing, and most specify the number of crew to be carried along with certain items of equipment such as a paddle, anchor, special buoyancy etc.

Since dinghies cannot race round a track like motor cars, the course for each race has to be set out beforehand. This is done with a series of marks, usually floating buoys. For open meetings and above it is usual to set a so-called Olympic-style course. For local races, the course is selected using some of several fixed buoys which the club will have available to it.

How Races are Run

Dinghies start by sailing across the starting line. This will be an imaginary line on the water drawn between two buoys. If the clubhouse is situated on a river or creek, the line is between two posts on opposite sides. If there is no opposite bank, the line is the extension of the transit between two posts set up on the shore.

The start of the race is indicated by a sound signal and a flag signal given at a designated time. Warning and preparatory signals are made at set intervals before the starting signal and to enable competitors to make a timed approach to the start line, so that they reach it just as the starting signal is made.

Handicap Racing

Normally, the first to finish wins the race, but if dinghies of different classes are competing it may be necessary to allocate each with a handicap. This is called 'handicap racing'. The time to complete the course by each competitor is recorded, the handicap applied and what is called the corrected time worked out. The winner is the competitor with the lowest corrected time.

Signals

The signals to be used in the race will be given in the sailing instructions, but the most common are laid down in the racing rules (IYRR 4). The following are those most likely to be encountered.

Signals are made by flags accompanied by a sound signal, but it is important to remember that under the rules (IYRR 4.7) times are always taken from the visual signal.

The class flag is flown as the warning signal, usually ten minutes before start time.

The Start

There are three types of start: the fixed line start, the committee boat start and the gate start. On a fixed line the wind might be blowing from any direction relative to the course to the first mark, but on a committee boat start things should have been arranged so that the course to the first mark is a beat. Gate starts are covered on the opposite page.

Line Start

The priorities on a line start are to arrive on the line at gunfire, going fast, in clear air and with no one close alongside (or even worse slightly in front) to leeward.

The boat handling skills needed most are the ability to sail slowly but in perfect control, the ability to accelerate quickly and the ability to judge distance in terms of time: how far will your boat travel in five seconds, in 30 seconds, or one minute?

Answering Pennant
Races postponed indefinitely.

AP with shape
Races postponed 15 minutes. Additional 15 minutes for each shape added.

'Round The Ends' starting rule in force.

L
There is an amendment to the sailing instructions *or* (on committee boat) 'Follow Me.'

N
All races are abandoned. If shown with class flag applies only to that class.

S

Shorten course. If shown at start means 'sail the short course'; if at end of round means 'finish at end of this round'; if on a committee boat near a mark means 'finish between committee boat and mark'.

1st Sub
General recall.

Red flag
Leave all marks to port

Green flag
Leave all marks to starboard.

Blue flag
This committee boat is on station on the finish line.

All these skills can only be acquired by practice.

Where to Start on the Line

On a fixed line, there will nearly always be a favoured or windward end. Other things being equal, that is the best place to start, but there might be reasons for avoiding it.

If the line is heavily favoured there will be an enormous crush at the windward end with the risk of being forced over the line early, luffed the wrong side of the pin (outer limit) or even involved in a collision.

Inevitably you will be very close to other boats with all the problems of disturbed air that result. One boat from the bunch might make a great start, but the others will just be in each other's way. It can pay to start a little to leeward of this bunch, but you must be going fast and close to the line when the gun goes. While they sort themselves out, you are clean away.

Timing the Approach

Since the line is created only at the last minute in a gate start, you cannot do practice runs at it to get the feel of approaching the line. However, on a fixed or committee vessel line, the line should be laid well before the start and you can do some practice runs.

Pick a spot from where you think you might want to start and where you can see a mark to fix your position: a boat moored close by, a transit on shore or something similar. See how long it takes you to sail from there to the line.

In this way, you can give yourself a guide to exactly where your dinghy should be with one minute to go, two minutes to go, and so on.

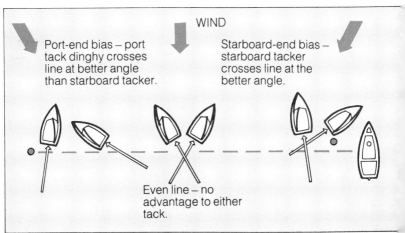

WIND

Port-end bias – port tack dinghy crosses line at better angle than starboard tacker.

Starboard-end bias – starboard tacker crosses line at the better angle.

Even line – no advantage to either tack.

Establishing which end of the line is favoured is vital in knowing where to start, but with a heavy bias it might be best to avoid the congestion at that end.

Committee Boat Start

On a committee boat line, establish which end is favoured either by using your compass or by sailing along the line with mainsail trimmed perfectly and traveller centred. Keep mainsheet and traveller cleated, tack and sail back along the line. If the mainsail luffs you are sailing towards the favoured end, if the mainsail is now sheeted too close you are sailing away from the favoured end. If the mainsail is correctly trimmed, the line is square across the wind and neither end is favoured.

Approaching the Start

As gun time approaches, sail slowly towards the line, making sure that you are close enough to be able to lay across the line close hauled, but not so close that you might be luffed over by boats coming up from leeward. If someone tacks under your bow, slow down to let them get clear, or speed up to sail over them.

Watch out for boats coming in from weather and blanketing you. Avoid starting in the middle of the line if a round-the-ends rule applies. If you are over early you will have a long way to go before being able to start properly.

Gate Start

In a gate start, a dinghy known as the pathfinder sails close hauled on port tack away from the leeward end buoy of the start line, followed by a small committee boat known as the gate launch. When the gun goes, dinghies may start anywhere between the buoy and the stern of the launch. After gunfire the pathfinder keeps going for some minutes, the gate launch following and the line thus grows longer.

The angle of the line is that of a dinghy on port tack and in theory there is no difference in starting early and getting away up the course or starting late and being further to windward but behind. In practice early starting pays if the wind shifts left, heading starboard tack and lifting port. Starting late pays if the wind shifts right, giving a lift to those on starboard tack.

Rules that Apply Especially at Start Time

Under the rules, all boats, be they dinghies or ocean racers, are called yachts and the rules apply to all yachts once they are racing. This is taken to be from the preparatory signal which in all general cases is the five-minute signal. A yacht ceases to be racing once she has finished, retired or the race has been called off. (Part 1, Definitions).

A yacht clear astern has to keep clear of a yacht clear ahead (37.2). When the yacht clear astern overlaps the yacht clear ahead one of them becomes the windward and one the leeward yacht; the windward yacht has to keep clear of the leeward yacht (37.1) but the leeward yacht may not unduly prevent her from doing so and must give her time to get out of the way (37.3 and 35).

Before starting you may luff as you please (40) except that you may not go above close hauled if the windward yacht is forward of mast abeam. If your luff affects more than one other (often the case before starting) you may not go above close hauled unless all are aft of mast abeam (40 and 38.6).

If any of the yachts to windward hail 'mast abeam', you must respect the hail even if you disagree and protest if you think fit (38.4). Since there is no proper course before starting, you only have to bear away on to a close hauled course (40) to fulfil your obligations.

The normal mark-rounding rules do not apply to a starting mark surrounded by navigable water. This means you cannot claim water on dinghies to leeward of you at the starting mark and if you try to reach in and round it you may be forced out. By the same rule you do not have to give room to anyone trying to do this, but once the gun has gone you may not squeeze someone out if you have to luff above close hauled to do it, or above the compass course to the next mark if the course is not a beat.

If you are trying to squeeze someone out and the gun goes, you must immediately bear away on to close hauled or on to the course for the next mark. If you are both already above the line to the starting mark, you only have to bear away on to that line (Rule 42.4)

After a general re-call or at a big meeting the round-the-ends rule (51.1c) may apply. This means that if you are over the line at any time in the minute before the start, you may only start by going round one of the ends of the starting line. Code flag I is flown during this minute.

If Code Flag I is not flying and you are over the line you may retrieve the situation simply by dipping back across the line and starting correctly (51.1b) but until you have started correctly, you must keep clear of all yachts which have started or which are already on the correct side of the line but have not started (44).

Know the Rules
Throughout this section, it is possible only to give general guidance on which rules apply when. Anyone who goes dinghy racing is strongly urged to acquire and study a copy of the complete racing rules, called *Thè International Yacht Racing Rules 1985–88.*

Beating

Sail Trim
Whole books have been written about sail trim and there is only room here for the basic rules of thumb. Sail trim when going to windward is a continuing compromise, a compromise between pointing high, that is, close to the wind, and sailing fast.

Generally speaking, the higher you point, the slower you go. This is fine provided that what you lose in speed you more than gain in distance saved by sailing closer to the line to the weather mark, but another element comes into the equation. As your dinghy slows down the centreboard becomes less efficient and the dinghy makes more leeway.

The more you pin in the sails, the flatter and less twisted they become and the higher you can point, but the less power they produce. The more you ease the sails, the fuller and more twisted they become and the more power they develop but the lower you can point.

In medium winds and in flat water, pointing ability can be maximized, since the strength of the wind will drive the boat fast and there are no waves to stop her. In light winds speed just to move through the water must be maintained at the expense of pointing ability, while in waves power will be needed to force the dinghy through the seas.

Setting the Jib

The controls are the jib sheet and the fairlead, with the halyard playing some part. The harder the halyard is set the tighter is the luff (this helps pointing ability) but the more rounded becomes the very front of the luff which can detract from pointing ability. Therefore, avoid over-tightening the halyard.

Moving the fairlead position forward decreases twist in the top of the sail, moving it back increases twist. Moving it forwards rounds out the lower part of the sail but it also closes the slot between the leech of the jib and the leeward side of the mainsail. This slot is very important as it allows the air flowing over the jib to escape – and the faster the airflow over the sails, the faster goes the boat. In some classes it is possible to adjust the fairlead athwartships: moving it inboard narrows the angle of attack of the jib (which increases pointing ability) but at the same time closes the slot.

Easing sheet tension (we are talking here of half-inches, not the big adjustments used when altering course) makes the sail more full, which increases power. Hardening sheet tension flattens the sail which gives less power but increases pointing ability.

Trimming the Mainsail

The controls are the halyard and cunningham, the kicking strap (kicker), the traveller and the mainsheet. The halyard works the same way as the jib halyard but because the main has a longer and more stretchy luff and because class rules normally limit the maximum length of mainsail luff on the mast (the black

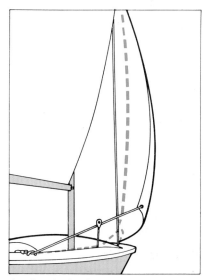

Letting the barber hauler up (solid line) lifts the clew and twists the sail.

bands), the cunningham is used in conjunction with the halyard to adjust luff tension.

The kicker controls the vertical angle of the boom: if the kicker were not there and the mainsheet were eased, the boom would rise up as well as go out. It also affects mast bend lower down, by pulling the boom forwards against the mast as the kicker is tensioned. Finally, the kicker can be used to flatten the lower part of the mainsail by bending the boom in the middle.

The traveller (when fitted) controls the horizontal angle of the boom in conjunction with the mainsheet and is used with the mainsheet to adjust the amount of twist in the sail. For example, traveller down and mainsheet hard gives a light leech to the mainsail with little twist; traveller high and mainsheet soft gives a slack leech to the mainsail with a lot of twist.

Once the mainsheet has been set, the traveller can be moved up or down its track to adjust the angle of attack of the mainsail without altering the amount of twist.

See How They Work
Go sailing and make all these adjustments one by one, over-tightening and over-easing each control in turn and watching the effect on the sails. It is all much easier to see than read about.

Telltales
The jib should have telltales at one-third, half and two-thirds the luff height. The mainsail should have a telltale on the end of each batten

pocket. Telltales show how the wind is flowing over the sails: across the luff of the jib there should be an even flow all the way up and on both sides, causing the telltales to stream aft, horizontally. If the windward telltales begin to drop you are pinching: bear away a bit. If the leeward telltales start to rotate or to drop, you are too free: come up a bit.

If the upper telltales break before the lower telltales, there is too much twist in the sail; move the sheet lead forward: vice versa if the lower telltales break first.

On the jib, it helps always to stick the starboard telltale a little above the height of the port telltale in each pair: that way you can easily tell which is which when the sun is shining through the sail and you can see both quite easily.

On the mainsail all the telltales should stream aft together, but the most important is the top. If it doesn't stream, adjust the twist until it does.

Basic Trimming Rules
Flat Water, Medium Winds. Sails should be trimmed as close as possible for high pointing. Jib lead

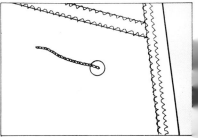

Telltales should be 3–4 ins (8–10 cm) from the luff, starboard above port.

should be at its most inboard setting, sheet tension fairly hard, jib lead fairly well forward to give less twist but full bottom to sail and close slot. Main traveller should be on centreline or a little to windward, mainsheet fairly well tensioned but not at maximum. Little or no twist in mainsail, boom on centreline.

Flat Water, Light Winds. Fullness needed in sails to give power, but don't overdo it. In very light airs too much fullness gives the airflow too far to travel round the sail: 0–3 knots of breeze, keep sails flat; 3–6 knots of breeze, sails full; above 6 knots, pointing ability is obviously suffering. Use more twist than in medium winds.

Choppy Water, Medium Winds. Power is needed to drive the boat through the chop. Start easing the

Britain's Cathy Foster, the only woman in the world ever to win a race at the Olympic Games, demonstrates perfect boat and sail trim in her 470.

A 470 crew maintain good upright trim for fast upwind sailing.

traveller down and moving the jib lead outboard to open the slot; do not try to point as high as in flat water.

Waves and Heavy Winds. Plenty of twist needed to de-power the top of the rig and reduce heeling moment. Traveller should be right down as most of the time the main will be lifting or the dinghy would be over-powered. Jib lead open and aft.

Boat Trim

Dinghies are designed to be sailed upright, yet this is very difficult to do. When most crews think they have the boat upright there is still 5% or more of heel to leeward. To check, look at the horizon over the transom, not the bow, and keep the

top of the transom level with th horizon. Look too at the wake: there is more disturbance on th leeward side of the wake as it leave the transom and rudder, the boat heeled to leeward.

In general, keep weight in th middle of the boat fore-and-aft, th two of you close together. In lig winds, keep the weight a little fo ward to lift the transom clear of th water and in very light airs (0 to knots) the dinghy should be pu posely heeled to leeward as we This reduces the wetted surfac area of the hull, lessening drag, an also helps keep the sails in the proper shape.

As waves appear, move th weight aft a little to lift the bo

ightly and make the dinghy easier steer, but not so much that the ow can be thrown off to leeward as wave hits it.

entreboard

very light winds, angle the cen-
eboard forward by as much as 5°.
his increases pointing ability and
oves the centre of lateral resist-
ice of the underwater part of the
inghy forward, which in turn in-
ices slight weather helm and gives
e rudder some feel. As soon as the
reeze picks up, move the cen-
eboard to vertical, or weather
elm will increase dramatically. In
eavy winds, rake the centreboard
t by 5° or even more to help
educe weather helm.

eering in Waves

significant wave to a dinghy sailor
one that is the same height as the
inghy's freeboard. When waves
each this height you must think of

how best to steer over or round them to keep speed up. The slowest route is through the wave.

Since luffing up slows the dinghy down it is usually quickest to bear away over and round waves, but there are exceptions especially when coping with really big waves, i.e. those where you can only see the sails of boats not in the same trough as yourself.

In big waves, luff slightly as you climb the face of the oncoming wave

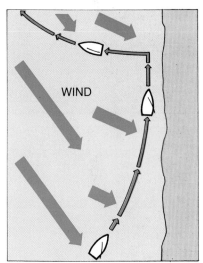

Above: There is often a lift along the shore where the wind bends to cross the beach.

then bear away just as you reach the top, so that the boat does not fall off the wave on the other side. Always try to keep speed on: as you slow-down, leeway increases and if you stop you greatly increase the risk of capsize.

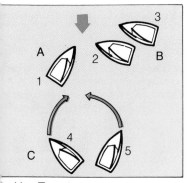

acking Together

Port tack boat 1 keeps clear of 2.
3 (windward boat) keeps clear of 2.
4 keeps clear of 5, on his right side.

Rules that Apply Especially When Beating

A dinghy on port tack must keep out of the way of one on starboard tack (36). A dinghy to windward keeps clear of one to leeward (37). This means that if the boat to leeward is pointing higher than you and gradually closes the gap, you must tack-off to keep clear.

When two boats are tacking together, the one on the right of the pair will normally have right-of-way during the tack (41.4) and after the tack (it will be starboard tack).

Simple Tactics

Spotting windshifts is the hardest part of sailing to windward. Even in a steady breeze, the wind direction will oscillate up to 5° or 10° either side of the mean direction. Watching the compass is the easiest way to spot such a shift: if the numbers increase while on port tack, you are being headed, if they decrease you are being lifted. The opposite is the case on starboard tack.

The basic rule is tack when headed – but don't rush it. Wait at least half a minute to ensure that the header is genuine. This is especially true when sailing in waves where you cannot hold a steady course.

Beware the velocity headers. As the wind lightens in strength, the forward-movement component in the apparent wind equation is increased until the boat loses speed to match the lower wind strength. This causes the apparent wind to swing forward, giving the appearance of a heading shift. In fickle winds this can be quite large. If you are headed, make sure it is not just the wind lightening before you tack. If you d tack you will find yourself headed c the other tack as well and you wi lose speed because of the tack.

Wind Bends

In onshore wind conditions, the wind usually bends as it approaches th shore so as to cross the shoreline a right angles. This gives a lift along the shore when you are sailing to wards the shore, and a header a you come away from the shore. Th wind will also tend to bend round headland, following the line of th coast.

Wind Swings

These can be caused by the weath er system in operation and will usu ally be forecast (backing is swingin

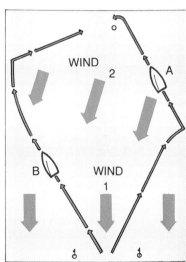

By sailing towards the windshift, A sails a shorter distance than B.

to the left, or anticlockwise; veering is swinging to the right). It is surprising how often the forecasters are right. Wind swings can also be caused by an onshore breeze being augmented by a sea breeze as it builds during the day. As the land heats up it sucks in wind off the sea. The more this happens, the more the breeze will blow onshore at right angles to the general lie of the coastline, and the breeze will increase in strength.

Which Way to Go

Having decided what you think the wind is going to do, you must sail the boat accordingly. If there is an identifiable bend to the wind, sail towards the bend. If you think the wind is going to swing, sail towards the direction in which the wind will swing: i.e. if the wind is going to swing to the right (veer), sail towards (and then stay on) the right-hand side of the course.

However, avoid getting too far out on a limb unless you think you know something the others do not. If you are not sure, or if you are sure there are no swings and bends, stay in the middle, tacking on the shifts, and stay off the laylines. Once out on the layline to the weather mark, you are committed and have no more room for manoeuvre.

A starboard-hand rounding means that a starboard-tack approach entails a tack around the mark: 14 cannot tack until 13 has done so.

The Weather Mark

Approaching the Mark (Port-hand rounding)

Having avoided the laylines for most of the beat, you now have to get on to a layline in order to round the mark. Ideally you should approach the mark on the starboard tack, to give right-of-way over boats coming in on port. You therefore only have to bear away, not tack, round the mark. But the further out you hit the starboard tack layline, the harder it is to judge exactly when to tack for the mark. The ideal distance is about 100–150 feet (30–50 m), not difficult to judge but time enough for the crew to set the spinnaker pole.

This ideal can be messed up by other boats. Arriving in a bunch, all the dinghies tack a little to the weather side of the one ahead to keep clear wind. Soon, the result is a long echelon of starboard-tack dinghies, most of whom have overstood the mark. Here is a chance for the sailor who stayed inside the layline to pick up many places by deliberately understanding the mark on starboard, coming in on port and tacking under the bow of a boat already laying the mark. To do this, of course, you have to be good at tacking and accelerating your boat and be a good judge of distance and speed.

Approaching the Mark (Starboard-hand Rounding)

The same basic rules apply, but the situation is complicated by the fact that a starboard tack approach involves a tack round the mark. Even approaching on starboard, you lose your right-of-way on port tack boats as soon as you commence your tack, while once you have tacked you will be on port and vulnerable to starboard tack boats who were astern but to weather. Fine judgement is essential and there it can pay to overstand a boat's width or so.

Remember too that coming away from the mark you will be on port and must keep clear of starboard tackers still approaching the mark.

Rules that Apply Especially at Mark Roundings

(Rule numbers are given in brackets) The port-and-starboard rule (36) dominates the mark rounding – hence the starboard tack approach – but another very important rule is the Changing Tacks rule (41). When tacking you must keep clear of other boats which are on tack (41). The tack commences when you are beyond head to wind and (since you are beating) is complete when you

Port-hand rounding: the starboard-tack approach does not entail a tack at the mark and is much safer.

are on a close-hauled course, irrespective of what your sails are doing or how fast you are going (Part 1, Definitions).

This definition is very important especially in starboard-hand roundings since it means the starboard tack dinghy still has right-of-way until the moment she is head to wind. She can shoot up to the mark and port tack boats must keep clear under rule 36. Meanwhile the starboard tack boats astern or to windward must keep clear under rule 37 unless so close to the mark as to have an overlap (42). She may not, however, shoot up like this to prevent a starboard tack yacht, clear ahead, from tacking round the mark (42.2(b)).

If making a port tack approach to tack on to starboard (see port-hand roundings) you must tack clear of the starboard tack boats, but as soon as your tack is complete – and in a dinghy this happens very quickly (*Definitions* – dinghies astern or to windward must keep clear of you).

As long as the boat astern did not have to start taking avoiding action before your tack was complete, you are clear (41.2) even though he may have to take avoiding action moments later because of his extra speed.

The Rounding
Do not forget to leave room at the mark to enable you to bear away and, in particular, to ease the mainboom out. If the next leg is going to be a very close reach, you can afford to come in to the mark high and slightly overstood, for you will

want to go high on the next leg a be to weather of the dinghies ahe and astern. As the dinghy a proaches the mark, the crew sho set the spinnaker pole unless ma rounding entails a tack or a gybe. the dinghy rounds the mark, ea the main and jib sheets and set t centreboard for the next leg.

Reaching

Setting the Spinnaker
The spinnaker is just a sail like a other. There is no need to be afra of it, but setting it, in particul require some practice. The sp naker is usually rigged and put in chute or basket before launchi the boat so that, to set it, all you ha to do is pull a few strings.

Free the sheet and guy from the stowed and cleated positions so th each is free to run. The crew se the spinnaker pole by clipping t guy through the hook on the po end, pushing the pole out to hang the topping lift and clipping t other end of the pole to the ring the mast. The jib should be hook under the reaching hook at t shroud if the next leg is to be reach.

To hoist the spinnaker, the helm man stands up and steers with t tiller between his knees and ha the halyard while the crew tends t sheet and guy. As the sail comes c of the chute or bag, haul hard on t

Right: A Fireball blasts down the reach at full speed.

guy to pull the tack of the spinnaker to the pole and pull the luff clear of the jib to allow the spinnaker to fill, then trim the sheet.

If the spinnaker is coming out of a bag at the aft end of the foredeck it can help to keep the jib sheeted close so it does not slow the spinnaker up; if launching from a chute the jib should be sheeted free or even let flap to help the spinnaker fill quickly.

Once the spinnaker is full, the crew takes the sheet and guy while the helmsman trims main and jib and steers the boat down the reach.

Trimming the Spinnaker

The simple rules for trimming the spinnaker are:
* Keep the pole as far aft as possible; this is usually at right angles to the wind direction
* Keep the sheet eased as far as it will go without allowing the luff of the spinnaker to fold in and collapse.
* Keep the tack and the clew of the spinnaker level horizontally: since the clew will fly at its own level, the height of the outboard end of the pole must be adjusted using the topping lift and downhaul to

To promote planing, the crew use their weight to get the dingy level.

put the tack at the same level a the clew.

Boat Trim

How we trim the dinghy on a reac depends on whether or not she w plane. On a light airs reach wher there is no question of planing, trir is much as for going to windward.

Once the dinghy is planing, cre weight has to be kept further aft t stop the bow going in and buryinc bringing the dinghy off the plane Do not, however, move weight to far aft or move weight aft too earl) The simple test is to look at th wake. If the weight is building u round the rudder, the dinghy is nc planing and all that weight aft i doing is digging the stern in, caus ing excessive drag.

Once the dinghy is planing, th wake as it comes off the transom i smooth and flat, hissing satisfactorily with the rudder blade throwing up feathery tail of spray. This is why yo sail dinghies in the first place. Th sensation, once experienced, is un mistakable and there are few thing in life to beat it.

Promoting Planing

Much fun and many places can be won by coaxing the dinghy on to the plane earlier than everyone else and in marginal planing condition: this is how to do it. First, keep the boat absolutely level (see page 58) Luff up slightly above the course i the lulls: this keeps the apparen wind on or forward of the beam anc keeps the dinghy moving quickl) through the light patches.

When a gust comes, bear away

out 15° and ease and trim both
ainsheet and jib sheet rapidly, at
e same time leaning aft. As you
el her lift on the plane, slide your
eight about a foot (30 cm) aft along
e sidedeck and concentrate hard
a sail trim and keeping her upright.
the gust does not last you will feel
er come off the plane and the wake
stead of hissing will start to bubble
d gurgle again: luff up, trim and
ove forward, ready for the next
ıst.

sing Waves

ou can derive much help from
aves. Reaching, the waves will run
cross your course from windward
leeward. As a crest approaches,
ear away so that it lifts the stern
d the dinghy starts to surf down
e wave. Once she is going, luff up
gain across the wave to use its face
r the maximum time. As you reach,
e bottom of the wave passes under
ou. Bear away again to climb on to
e next wave.

Rules that Apply Especially on the Reaching Legs

(Rule numbers are given in brackets)

The most commonly encountered
rule on this leg is that concerning
luffing (38). Since under rule 37 a
windward boat must keep clear of a
leeward, the leeward can luff (see
Definitions) to try and prevent a
windward boat from overtaking her
to windward.

In fact, luffing seldom pays, yet
there are some sailors – usually at
the back of the fleet – who will luff
you to Kingdom Come if they get the
chance. The leeward yacht cannot
luff if at any time during the overlap
the windward boat has been forward of mast abeam (38.2): this rule
prevents a dinghy overtaking
another to leeward above her
proper course. She can luff as many
boats as she likes, provided she has
rights on them all (38.6).

Note that the proper course is not
necessarily a direct line to the next

he leading GP14 may have to luff to avoid being overtaken to windward.

mark: it is the quickest route, and this might be affected, in particular, by tidal or current considerations. Mast abeam is defined (38.2) as the windward helmsman sitting in his normal position and sighting abeam while sailing no higher than the leeward yacht, being abeam or forward of the mast of the leeward yacht. This is a good deal further forward than many people imagine. The leeward dinghy can luff until the windward dinghy has reached the mast abeam position and it is up to the helmsman of the windward dinghy to call 'mast abeam' (38.4).

Beware of hailing too early: the leeward dinghy has to bear away on to her proper course as soon as the hail is made, but can protest if the hail was improper. Other important rules on this leg are the overlap rule (38.6) which defines when an overlap begins and rule 39, which prevents you sailing below your proper course to stop someone overtaking to leeward.

The Gybe Mark

Boat Handling
There is more high drama at the gybe mark than anywhere else on the course, but while certainly the gybe, especially in heavy weather, is one of the trickiest manoeuvres to perform in a dinghy   clear thinking and careful preparation can make life a lot easier.

The aim is to come away from the gybe mark in the best possible position. This will normally be clos to the mark, sailing as high or highe than the course for the next leg an to weather of the opposition. Ideall this means completing the gybe a or just before the mark. Ground wi be lost to leeward if you are st sorting the boat out after the mark

For the final 150 feet (50 metres into the mark, aim high so that you final 60 feet (20 metres) is on a broa reach or even a run. This eases th gybe and also means less danger c a capsize as the helmsman and cre move inboard to handle the sheet With the spinnaker, cleat the gu and sheet, unhook the guy from th reaching hook and then pull th weather jib across to gybe the jib.

Cleat the mainsheet for the ne reach, bear away on to a run, gra the whole part of the mainsheet an pull the boom across, turning th boat with the tiller. As the boor comes cross, give the tiller a quic flick the other way to stop the tur and straighten the dinghy. At th moment of the gybe and immedi ately afterwards you should b steering straight downwind.

Once the boat is under contro unclip the spinnaker pole from th mast, pull it across and clip it ove the old sheet which now become the new guy. Unclip it from the olo guy which thus becomes the nev sheet and clip it to the mast, pushin the pole out and forwards as you do The crew takes the spinnaker shee and away you go.

Tactics Against Other Boats
Seldom can we take the gybe mar irrespective of other boats. The ap

roach must be planned to try and et the inside berth (overlap) on oats ahead without giving away an verlap to boats astern. The crucial stance (see Rules Section) is two oats' length from the mark – that is hen the boat ahead enters the two-ngths circle if you are trying for an erlap.

There are two methods of attack. ou can try blanketing the boat in ont to slow him down, then dive to eward for the overlap at the cru-al moment; or you can sail lower an the boat ahead, luffing up to ain speed and the inside berth just s you approach the mark.

The first method can only be used the reach is broad. If the reach is ly you will be so far up alongside m before your blanket takes effect at you will not be able to bear vay under his stern.

The second method can work on broad or close reach, but on a very ly reach luffing up will not give fficient increase in speed. How-ver, on a shy reach it can still work, you can trick him into going very gh, because as the windward boat rns to come down to the mark, he ens the distance in which it is ossible to gain an overlap on him.

he Leeward Mark

n an Olympic-type course the lee-ard mark is approached either om a reach, on the reaching laps, from a run. In club racing the me applies even though the rest of e course may not have been a roper Olympic triangle, except at rounding the mark might in-lve a gybe.

Approaching on a Reach

This is the simplest case. All we have to do is take down the spin-naker, pull the plate right down and harden up round the mark. There is usually no difficulty breaking margi-nal overlaps. Luff up early (the better established the overlap the earlier you have to start luffing) thus forcing the weather boat to come with you. Then, just before you reach the two-lengths circle, bear away hard. Since an overlap is judged at right-angles to the line of your transom as you enter the two length circle you will probably break the overlap.

Approaching on a Run

This is the more difficult approach because on a run you are going at your slowest, while those astern can blanket your sails and come up on you and those on either side can gain speed by luffing across you. Attack and defence on the run are dealt with on page 75.

Assuming there are no problems from other boats, aim to leave the mark wide on the approach side, passing as close as you dare as you round and coming away from the mark as far to windward as possible. In particular do not leave room for a boat astern to follow you round and finish up on your weather quarter.

Rules that Apply Especially at the Gybe Mark

(Rule numbers are given in brackets.)

Rule 42 deals with rounding marks and establishing overlaps. It is a complicated rule and should be studied in full. 42.1 states that any yacht rounding the mark shall give room to any yacht which has an inside overlap on her, provided the overlap was established before the leading yacht's bow was within two lengths of the mark (2.3a(ii)). Once the overlap is thus established, the inside yacht is entitled to room even if the overlap is subsequently broken – for example by accelerating on a wave (42.3c) but she cannot do just as she pleases: she must give the outside yacht room to keep clear (35) and must gybe at the first reasonable opportunity unless she has luffing rights over all the yachts outside her (42.1b). If no overlap

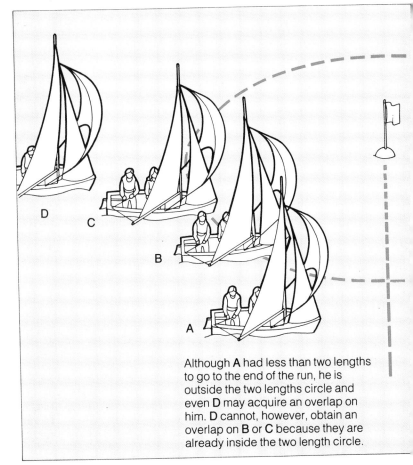

Although **A** had less than two lengths to go to the end of the run, he is outside the two lengths circle and even **D** may acquire an overlap on him. **D** cannot, however, obtain an overlap on **B** or **C** because they are already inside the two length circle.

xists or is established, yachts clear stern must give yachts clear ahead oom to round the mark (37.2 and 2.2a).

After the gybe, you may only sail bove the proper course if you have uffing rights on all the boats to veather (38.2) but whether or not ou have luffing rights is decided om the moment your gybe is com-lete (38.3).

ounding with a Gybe

'his situation often arises in club acing, or on an Olympic course, specially if there has been a wind-hift or your downwind tacking has ft you with an oblique approach to ie mark. The only real problem is etting the spinnaker down and way early, so that the boat is tidy nd ready for the beat as you round ie mark.

Aore about Overlaps

Because of the slower speeds and lownwind approach, there is more verlap trouble at the leeward mark han anywhere else.

If a dinghy clear astern is fol-owing to the mark and looks like vinning an overlap, try aiming to eeward of the mark. Harden up just efore two-lengths and there is a good chance that you'll break the verlap.

Avoid being stuck on the outside f a line of boats hardening up for he mark. As you turn towards the nark you will be outside the two engths circle, but the action of your urning to the mark will open an verlap on all the boats inside you ven though they were well behind

before you turned. A dinghy with her sails spread out for running is almost as wide as she is long, so if you are number three or more in the line abreast you are vulnerable to this attack.

Conversely, you can gain an overlap in this way by staying on the rhumb line (shorter distance) to the mark and getting to the two-length circle before the boats outside – but be prepared for a bitter argument: few people realise how they can give away an overlap like this. Rule 42 is the one to know by heart.

Running

Tacking Downwind

The first thing to be said about running is that it is slow, so as far as possible don't do it. When a dinghy is running, her sails are at their least efficient – she is just being blown along by the wind instead of using the airflow to develop power. In addition, she is sailing directly away from what wind there is, so the apparent wind she feels is very low – and the faster she tries to sail away from the wind, the slower becomes the apparent wind. Sailing across the wind, her speed works with the wind speed to keep the speed of the apparent wind high.

So in nearly all cases it pays to reach across the course, gybe and reach back. Even though greater distance is covered, the dinghy travels at greater speed. Obviously it is possible to overdo this. There comes a point where the greater

Fireballs approach the end of the run at a championship meeting.

speed no longer compensates for the greater distance. This varies from class to class and with the wind strength. The general rules are that the lighter and faster the dinghy, the more speed can be gained by reaching up; while the lighter the wind, the more speed can be gained by reaching.

Great gains can be made by reaching up in marginal planing conditions, if the dinghy will plan on a broad reach but not on a run. Not for nothing is a course straight downwind known as a 'dead run'.

Shifts on the Run

Windshifts on the run are every bit as important as windshifts on the beat. They enable you to reach-up into the apparent wind but at the same time stay close to the rhumb

These young Cadet sailors have their dinghy well-trimmed and nicely balanced as they plane along on the downwind leg.

line. However in the same boat in light winds they might be sailing anything up to 70° to keep the boat moving.

A word of warning though: in very light winds when using big gybing angles, beware of straying so far from the rhumb line that you miss a new breeze coming in from the other side of the course.

Broad Reaching

Many downwind legs are not true runs but broad reaches. On an Olympic-style course this can be caused by a windshift, on a club course simply because none of the fixed marks will give a true run. Here the fastest route is to sail the rhumb line, luffing up in the lulls to keep speed and bearing away in the gusts to get back down to the course – or below it to give room to luff in the next lull.

Attack and Defence

Windshadow is the attacking weapon on the run and the initiative lies mainly with the boat astern. If you are astern, sail so that your racing flag or Windex points at the centre of your opponent's mainsail. If ahead, sail so that your wind is kept clear. If someone astern blankets you from weather, luff boldly across his bow to get clear air or gybe away. Don't just sit there and never, ever, luff slowly.

Luffing as a Defence

There are only two reasons for luffing: to keep your wind clear or to hit your opponent and thus disqualify him under rule 37. In both cases,

luffing slowly does not work. Keeping your wind clear, luff early to show you mean business. If your opponent has any sense he will stay below you, realising that as the two of you luff towards the horizon others will get through both of you to leeward. If he insists on coming, consider gybing away – by continuing the luffing match you will only lose places to boats to leeward and astern.

If you decide to 'take out' an opponent who insists on sailing close on your weather, here is how to do it. Warn your crew, quietly, to be ready to retrim the spinnaker and jib. Make sure the centreboard is down at least three-quarters. Suddenly and violently put the helm down, sheeting in the sails as you do so to keep up speed and stay ahead of his mast abeam position.

Don't shout or warn him – you are trying to hit him, not help him. You will normally have to alter course by about 45° to get him: altering too much may allow him to claim mast abeam. Since when he sees you coming he will almost certainly yell 'mast abeam' as a reflex, whether he is or not, you must not give him time.

Once you have made up your mind to luff someone out, don't mess around – do it, and do it hard. A half-hearted attempt will only let him off the hook and probably let him past you.

Rules that Apply Especially on the Run

(Rule numbers are given in brackets.)

The most commonly encountered

rule on the run is Rule 37 – windward boat keeps clear. Note that this only applies when dinghies are overlapped, but of course a dinghy clear astern must also keep clear. Many sailors think there is a rule that says 'overtaking boat keeps clear': this applies in ordinary sailing (the International Regulations for Preventing Collisions at Sea) but there is no such rule in racing.

If an overtaking dinghy establishes an overlap to leeward, the windward dinghy must keep clear of her, even if this means she now has to alter course – for example to keep her spread-out mainboom clear of the boat which has come inside her (37.1). However, the leeward dinghy must establish the overlap in such a way that the windward dinghy has both room and time to keep out of her way (37.3). The leeward (overlapped) dinghy may not sail above her proper course (38.2) until she pulls clear ahead or gybes and gybes back again or moves more than two boats' lengths away and comes back when ahead of mast abeam (38.3). Of course, when gybing and gybing back she is subject to rule 36 (port and starboard) and rule 41 (keeping clear while gybing). Finally, be sure that your spinnaker tack stays close to the pole end (54.3).

Finishing the Race

The race is not over until the finishing line is crossed, so it is important to keep concentrating all the time until you have finished.

Covering on the Final Beat

On the final leg of the course, it i̵ important to protect your hard-wo finishing position by covering thos astern. The self-evident way to d this is to stay between your oppo nents and the finish line. This is eas enough to do if the final leg is reach or close fetch, often the cas in club racing, but not so easy to d on a beat.

Beware of covering too closely: you tack on an opponent's wind h will almost certainly tack himsel This is fine if you want to force hin away from a particular side of the course or into an unfavourable wind shift but it may mean you have t tack yet again if all you want to do i stay with him.

You may have to cover severa opponents who may not oblige yo by all sailing in the same direction In this case stay midway betwee the two extremes of the two bunche and avoid being dragged to on wing of the course. If there is a ba windshift you might protect you position against one or two boats bu lose out to the half-dozen who are over on the other side of the shift The only time to allow yourself t devote all your attention to just one opponent is if you are racing each other for an overall place at the end of a series.

Approaching the Finish Line

The big question is – which end to go for? An unbiased finish line is extremely rare, so one end or the other will be favoured.

Assuming that the approach to the line is upwind (the case on an Olym

ic-type course, not always so on a
lub course) the leeward end of the
ne is the favoured end unless, from
our present position, you can fetch
ie windward end. Even then it may
ay to free off, gain extra speed and
o for the leeward end.

On an Olympic-type course the
ommittee will try to set the line at
ght angles to the rhumb line from
ie last mark – but of course the
vind will probably have shifted
.ightly, thus giving the line a bias.

On a normal course with port-
and marks a windshift to the right
veer) gives a bias to the pin end. A
vindshift to the left (backing) gives a
ias to the committee boat end.

oat for Boat Tactics at the Finish

is possible to pick up many places
t the finish. Having chosen your
nd, approach it as if it were the
indward mark. If the pin end is
voured, it can pay to underlay the
in on starboard, put in a short port
ick near the buoy and tack on to
arboard round the buoy. You can
ick up many places off boats finish-
g further up the line on starboard
ick in this way. If things are really
ght, and there are boats to leeward
nd ahead of you, give yourself
om to tack on to starboard to cross
ie line with right-of-way over those
oming in from the port-hand side of
ie course. However still aim to
nish on the buoy. Every boat-*width*
ou are up the line unnecessarily is
bout a boat-*length* you have given
vay in distance.

You can sometimes beat boats
head of you to the line by sailing
iem past the layline and then tack-

ing for the line yourself. Going for
the leeward end, you win the race
back to the pin. Going for the windward end, you force them to sail on
until they have overstood. They then
have to reach down to the line, thus
sailing a greater distance. Even if
one of them gains an overlap on you
at the mark or committee boat, your
bow will still be in front.

Rules to Watch Out for at the Finish
Beware of tacking on to port for the
windward end of the line slap in
front of a port-tacker who is bearing
away from you as starboard tack
boat (41). Unlike the windward end
starting mark, both committee boat
and finishing buoy are marks of the
course and the overlap rule (42)
applies.

If you are approaching the committee vessel but cannot clear it to
weather, would have to bear away
to avoid hitting it, and are prevented
from tacking by a boat close to
weather, you can call for room to
tack (43). The other boat must then
give you room either by tacking

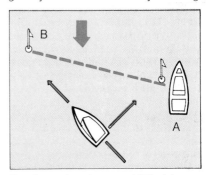

The Committee boat end (A) of the
finish line is nearer than the pin end (B).

herself or hailing 'you tack' (43.2).

However, if she herself can clear the committee vessel, she need not tack (but must tell you she can clear the vessel) (43.3a). If you hail again, she has to tack but you will be disqualified (43.3b). If, having refused to tack, she then does not clear the committee vessel, she must retire, accept a penalty, or you should protest her and she will be disqualified (43.3c).

The committee vessel is a mark of the course, but its anchor cable and any dinghies or boats tied up to it are not. You finish when your bow crosses the finishing line, but if after that you touch the finishing mark you must re-round it and 'finish' again.

Handling Protests

There is nothing sneaky or underhand about protesting, and it is a great pity that so many sailors speak of protests 'spoiling' racing. If you are touched by another dinghy you must either retire or protest (33.2) no matter how slight the contact. The race committee may decide that no further action need be taken if the contact was minor and unavoidable (33.3) but you do not have that right.

If you are touched by another boat, have to take action to avoid a collision when you have right of way or are otherwise involved in a rules incident, fly a protest flag (code flag B is the one – 68.2). Try to inform the other boat or boats that you will be protesting if they don't retire or take a penalty (68.4). When you get ashore, inform the race committee (68.6 or as altered by the sailing instructions).

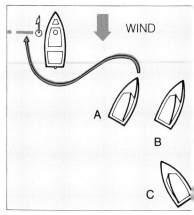

Above: **A** has carried **B** past the layline by preventing her from tacking and can tack on **C** and if necessary claim an overlap. Once **A** tacks, **B** will not have the speed to tack and establish an overlap on **A**.

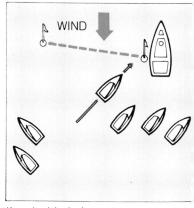

If undecided whom to cover approaching the finish, try and stay in the middle. If in doubt about which group is the greater danger, cover the larger group until the other group becomes obviously more dangerous

The protest committee will want ne protest in writing and before ney will even hear it will make sure ou followed all the steps above.

Full details of protest hearing pro-edures are in Part VI of the rules, ut in brief are as follows: you will e told when the hearing will occur 72.3); you have the right to be resent throughout the hearing 73.1); you can call witnesses and cross-examine the other party's wit-iesses to establish the facts – an mportant part of the process be-ause once the protest committee stablishes what it thinks are the acts, this decision is final (74.1) and annot be re-opened unless new vidence comes to light (73.5).

Once the evidence is taken, the rotest committee deliberate in pri-ate to find the facts and decide on vhat penalties to impose.

Racing in Britain

t is probable, although there are no eliable statistics to prove the matter ne way or the other, that the najority of sailing dinghies are used or racing. This is especially so in Britain. Perhaps this is because of he weather around the British coasts: in sunnier climes and with varmer water the particular incen-ive to go afloat that racing provides s not so necessary.

The vast majority of dinghy races are organized at local, club, level and are participated in by sailors vho have no desire to stretch them-selves further.

All clubs in Britain which run linghy racing must be affiliated to he Royal Yachting Association if they wish to use the International Yacht Racing Rules and participate in the dinghy class system, and for an individual to race it is necessary to belong to a recognized yacht or sailing club.

Taking up Racing

As mentioned previously under the heading 'Learning To Sail', most dinghy sailors come to racing by starting as crew, although it is poss-ible to buy a dinghy, attend a sailing school and then start racing without serving any sort of apprenticeship forward of the main thwart.

Many sailing schools, in addition to running basic courses, run courses on racing tactics, and if you decide to take dinghy racing seri-ously you might decide to join a class which organizes courses and seminars on racing techniques for itself. Many classes do this on a regular basis, and in Britain the National Sailing Centre at Arctic Road, Cowes, Isle of Wight will organize tailor-made courses either for classes or for clubs.

Youth Training

The RYA operates the National Youth Squad specificially to encour-age and train young people to race at every level from club to world championship. Begun in 1977, it has produced a number of world and European youth champions as well as World champions in general competition.

Youth Events are open to any competitor who has not had his or her 19th birthday, and who will not have it in the year of the event.

12017 is taking a risk by finishing
on port tack and may be caught on
the line by 11865 on starboard,
thus losing a place.

Part 3 Daysailing

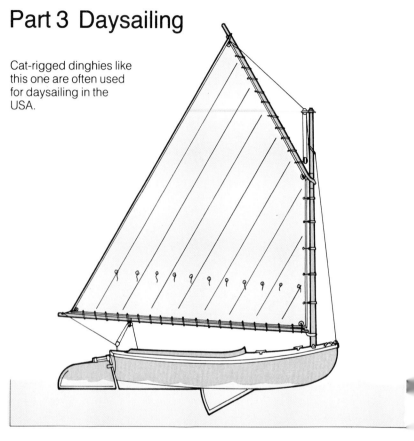

Cat-rigged dinghies like this one are often used for daysailing in the USA.

Not everyone who goes dinghy sailing goes racing; there is much pleasure to be had just pottering around. The majority of dinghies are genuinely dual-purpose and are suitable both for daysailing and racing, although of course some are more suitable than others. The big difference between the racing dinghy and the cruising dinghy will be in the amount of gear carried and in the layout of the boat.

For simple daysailing, fine tuning of the rig and sail trim are not so important, so there will be no need for extensive and elaborate control line layouts. However, space for picnic bags, thermos flasks and so on will be important, so if daysailing is your main aim, choose a boat with plenty of space for stowage.

Choose one, too, that does no have to be sailed as energetically as do many pure racing dinghies. Boats like the Wayfarer, GP 14, the Wanderer or any of the older, heavier local classes make excellent dual purpose dinghies. Boats such as the rascombe Lugger or the Mirror 16 ake excellent dayboats and are so suitable for camping and limed coastal cruising.

inghy Cruising

inghy cruising combines the fun and njoyment of camping with the added mension of being afloat and exploring the coast by small boat. Naturally, ecause of the size of the boats volved, the dinghy cruiser is more nited in the scope of his voyaging an is the yacht cruiser, but a dinghy can wriggle into nooks and crannies where no yacht could venture. Some dinghy cruising enthusiasts have made epic voyages in their boats, but most of us would be content with more modest ambitions.

One advantage of a dinghy is its great mobility on land, so your cruise need not involve a long voyage simply to reach your chosen holiday spot. That can all be done with the dinghy on a trailer behind the car: you launch when you arrive, load up the boat and off you go.

Shoal Waters, a 16 ft Fairey Falcon dinghy with a tiny cabin added, cruises ver 1000 miles each year under sail and oar, without the aid of a motor.

Daysailing and Camping

Some dinghy cruisers prefer to sleep ashore, unloading their tent and camping gear each evening and breaking camp next morning, or maybe operating from a base for a day or two of exploring and sailing before moving on. Others prefer to sleep and cook on board.

For this a suitable boom tent is required and can easily be made up to suit the exact measurements of your dinghy by a local sailmaker who also does covers and general canvas work.

If you want to live on board the dinghy, either at anchor overnight or hauled up on the beach, you'll need a boat at least 14 ft (4.27 m) long, preferably 16 ft (4.88 m) or 18 ft (5.5 m), and with sensible beam – 5 ft 10 in (2.1 m) is pretty much the minimum. You will also need a boat like the GP14, Wayfarer or Drascombe Lugger which has raised floorboards to keep your air bed and sleeping bags dry.

Naturally enough, keeping everything dry is a major concern when dinghy cruising.

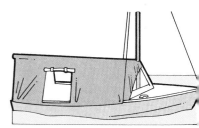

Above: For a cruising dinghy a boom tent can be made up to give camping accommodation

The Wayfarer will happily carry four adults for a pleasant day's sailing.

Navigation and Safety

rudimentary knowledge of navigation is an obvious requirement for anyone who wants to try dinghy cruising, but commonsense and the ability to read a chart or map are more important than the ability to use a sextant or even plot a fix. Since most dinghy cruising is done in rivers, in estuaries, or bay-hopping along the coast, you will normally either know where you are or establish your position by recognising features ashore from the chart.

You must know the state and run of the tides in your cruising area, both the times of high and low water (so you know when there will be water in a particular creek or alongside your chosen slipway) and the flow of the tidal stream. This you can read from the chart, so that you do not spend a frustrating day trying to sail against the current for six hours when you could be lounging on the beach waiting for the tide to turn or perhaps going the other way, where there is a nicer pub anyway.

And speaking of pubs, a detailed Ordnance Survey map of your chosen cruising ground will be of as much use as your nautical chart, for it will have much more detail of places of interest ashore.

Simple Safety Measures

In addition to the tent, the cooker, the food, the sleeping bags and all the personal gear, the daysailing and the cruising dinghy should be equipped with the following items:

anchor and cable
oars and rowlocks
two large scoop bailers
sails that can be reefed

This is by no means a complete list of all the items which the sensible cruising dinghy carries but it is an irreducable minimum without which you should not think of leaving the shore.

The anchor should be big enough to hold the dinghy overnight against a strong wind with the tide behind it. Avoid the folding grapnel type, it has insufficient holding power. The anchor cable should be a minimum of a fathom (two metres) of ³⁄₁₆in (5 mm) chain attached to 10 fathoms

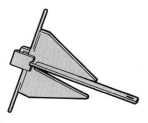

A Danforth pattern anchor which holds well in most conditions and will stow flat.

(18 m) of 12 mm diameter nylon warp. A separate warp of similar size should be carried as back-up, as a towing warp and as an extra mooring line.

Oars and rowlocks are preferable to paddles should you find yourself becalmed with the afternoon drawing into evening. Two large scoop bailers, tied into the boat with lanyards which are long enough to allow the bailers to be used without being untied, are necessary not just in case of capsize but in case waves come on board, or in case it rains heavily.

BEAUFORT SCALE FOR DINGHY SAILORS

Force	Wind Speed In mph	Description used in weather bulletins	
0	less than 1	Calm	Sea like a mirror, absolute drifting conditions. Racing sailors sit to leeward, heeling boat for minimum wetted surface; daysailers row or use the outboard.
1	1 to 4	Light Air	Catspaws, darker patches and ripples appear on surface. Dinghies move easily with one crew to leeward, one to windward. Burgee and telltales begin to work.
2	5 to 8	Light Breeze	Definite pattern to wavelets, easy to feel wind on cheek. Both crew to windward, racing sailors aware of pattern to windshifts.
3	8 to 12	Gentle Breeze	Waves beginning to form, occasionally with breaking tops: ideal dinghy sailing conditions with both crew sitting out but not too strenuously. Some water splashes aboard. Lightweight racing dinghies can plane on reaches.
4	13 to 20	Moderate Breeze	Waves becoming larger, most with breaking crests. White horses and occasional fóam on back of waves. Going to windward beginning to be hard work, trapeze crews out on wire with helmsman flat out. Risk of capsize especially with spinnaker or at gybe mark. Daysailers think about coming home, cruisers have reef in mainsail for beating
5	21 to 26	Fresh Breeze	Waves big enough to be a problem, stopping dinghy dead when going to windward. Much water coming on board unless great skill exercised when taking waves. Daysailers still at sea are usually making for home under jib only, many capsizes in racing fleet, rescue boats under pressure. Not everybody bothers with spinnaker, less than fully- experienced crews think twice about going afloat.

Force	Wind Speed in mph	Description used in weather bulletins	
6	27 to 33	Strong Breeze	Strictly for experts. Big waves at sea make progress difficult to windward, on inland waters trees and buildings cause sudden, slamming gusts. Very high speeds on reaches for those who can stay upright.
7	35 to 41	Near Gale	Survival conditions on open sea, expert conditions inland. Gear breakages frequent. Sea heaps up with breaking crests, long streaks of foam on wave backs. Dinghy cruisers try to have dinghy ashore and clear of the tide line rather than left at anchor.
8 9 10 11 12	42 to 80 and above	Gale. Strong Gale. Storm. Severe Storm. Hurricane.	Dinghies not tied down ashore likely to be blown over and damaged. Boat covers not firmly secured can be torn. Risk of general damage on land as wind increases.

A Fireball crew enjoy ideal Force 3 conditions.

Trailers and Trailing

Sooner or later you will want to take the dinghy on the road, away to an open meeting or a championship, or off on the start of the cruising holiday.

Choosing a Trailer
Putting the dinghy on a trailer and jolting it along behind a car are potentially very damaging things to do, so the first essential is a trailer which gives good support to the dinghy and carries it securely.

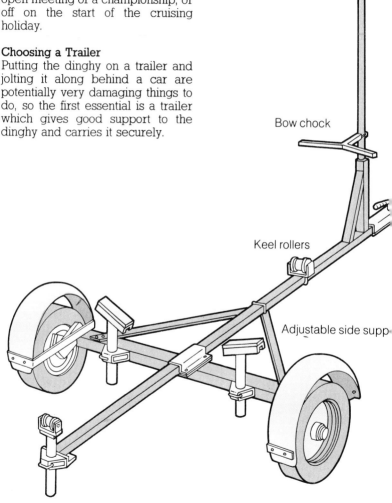

Mast support

Bow chock

Keel rollers

Adjustable side supp

A robust and simple road trailer. The weight of the dinghy is borne on the keel rollers with the side supports preventing rolling. Some lightweight dinghies are better in a moulded cradle which fits the hull shape.

Trailers for wood-built and conventional dinghies should take all the weight of the dinghy along the keel: the side supports are merely to steady the dinghy and stop her lolling sideways. In particular, there must be no weight on the bottom panels of the hull. on a wooden dinghy there is the risk that a jolt caused by a bump in the road could punch a hole in the bottom while even glassfibre hulls can be badly distorted by allowing the weight of the dinghy to be taken by the unsupported bottom panel.

Some modern dinghies such as the Laser have special trailers with moulded supports for the hull.

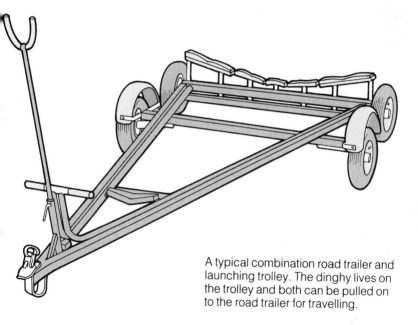

A typical combination road trailer and launching trolley. The dinghy lives on the trolley and both can be pulled on to the road trailer for travelling.

Combination Trailers

A conventional road trailer requires the dinghy to be lifted on and off her launching trolley for road journeys. This involves finding a way of taking the launching trolley along. A combination trailer is designed to carry the dinghy already on her launching trolley. Trailer and trolley are therefore bought together as one unit. Such an outfit greatly simplifies the chore of travelling with the dinghy and although more expensive than a conventional road trailer is worthwhile if you envisage taking the dinghy on road journeys more than once or twice a year.

Trailer Maintenance

Salt water is an enemy of a metal road trailer and especially of its wheel bearings. Avoid if at all possible putting the road trailer anywhere near the water. If you have to put the trailer in the sea, wash it off immediately with fresh water and change the grease in the wheel bearings. Do this by pumping fresh grease in through the grease nipple until all the old grease and with it the droplets of water in the bearing have been squeezed out the front. Never put the trailer straight into the sea after a long road journey: allow at least twenty minutes for the bearings to cool down. If you don't do this, the cold plunge causes the hot bearings to contract rapidly, sucking in salt water through the seals and rapidly causing the bearings to rust.

Check the bearings regularly for wear. Do this with the boat off the trailer by lifting each wheel in turn and giving it a spin. If the bearing rumbles or sounds gritty, all is not well. With the wheel off the ground, try and waggle it sideways: if there is any sideways movement the bearing is either loose or worn. A loose bearing can be tightened by removing the grease cap and tightening the large castellated nut on the spindle end, after first removing the split pin which goes through the hole in the spindle.

Tighten the nut until all play is removed and the wheel is beginning to feel stiff, then back it off to the next position where the split pin can be put through the hole in the spindle and the castellations on the nut.

Covers for Trailing

Remember that any cover used on the boat while trailing will have to withstand winds of up to Storm Force 10 (see page 87): a car towing at 50 mph (80 km/hr) into a moderate headwind can generate winds of Force 8 or 9. Trailing, the boat is bombarded with spray, small stones, and water laden with road dirt. For a racing dinghy especially an undercover is recommended, but it must be a snug fit and be properly secured. Otherwise the flapping cover could do more damage than the dirt and small stones it is intended to defeat.

Towing

Most modern cars will cope well with dinghies up to 19 ft (5.8 m), but the smaller and ligher the car, the greater will be the effect of boat and trailer. Remember also that it is not just the bare weight of the boat that must be considered, but also of all the gear: the sails, the sleeping bags, the outboard engine and so on. Using a small car to tow a heavy boat and trailer causes great wear on the clutch and can burn-out a small automatic.

The main driving differences with a trailer behind the car are increased braking distance and poorer acceleration, and the way in which the trailer cuts corners rather than following the same line as the car. Most dinghies and trailers are narrower than the towing car, but do not forget to allow for the extra height of the mast in its stowed position when using toll booths at bridges and tunnels, or entering utomatic car parks. Some automatic ar park barriers cannot cope with he extra length of boat and trailer nd the barrier arm comes down on he boat as you tow it through. This sually breaks the arm and doesn't elp the boat.

Beware of increased fuel consumption when towing: a car which might do 37 mpg might drop to 17 mpg when pulling a boat and railer. This is as much as 90 miles (145 km) less on one tankful of petrol. Thus allow for the need for extra fill-up points on your journey.

Allow extra time as well: anything from 30% more to double the normal time. You will not only be limited in speed but you may be stuck for much longer than normal behind slow-moving vehicles because of our inability to overtake.

Reversing

Reversing with a trailer is not as difficult as it looks. Find an empty car park and practice – in half-an-hour or less a competent driver will have mastered the basics. The simple rule-of-thumb is that the front of the car must be turned in the direction that the back of the trailer has to go. What you are doing is using the back of the car to push the front of the trailer, and the front of the trailer has to go the opposite way to the back to commence the turn.

The most common difficulty is oversteering while turning and thus jack-knifing car and trailer. Once you have started the trailer turning, straighten up. If the turn is not tight enough you can easily increase it

but the only way to reduce a too-tight turn is to stop, pull forward thus straightening car and trailer and then start again.

Be Prepared

Before towing any distance prepare a simple tools and spares kit and carry it in the car boot. It should include:
* Spare trailer wheel and tyre (inflated to correct pressure).
* A jack to lift the trailer (the car jack will not normally fit).
* Grease gun and tin of grease.
* Wheel spanner for trailer wheel nuts.
* Spare bulbs for trailer lighting board. To be sensible, also take:
* A spare set of wheel bearings or, better still, a complete hub unit with bearings.
* A complete set of socket spanners to fit all nuts on the trailer.
* Spare split pins.
* Rags and cleaning material.

Towing Abroad

You may wish to take your dinghy abroad with you on holiday. In EEC countries, generally speaking, if the trailer is legal in the country of registration it is also legal in the country being visited, except in the matter of width limits (a simple dinghy-and-trailer rig should cause few worries). Check with your motoring organization on the latest foreign regulations.

Remember also to have correct documentation for the dinghy so that you can get her in and out through both domestic and foreign customs.

Glossary

Abaft Behind, on the aft side of (used to describe position inside the boat).

Abeam Level with, alongside.

Aft Towards the stern.

Apparent wind The wind experienced by the boat moving across the water. It is a combination of the 'true wind' and the wind created by the boat's movement.

Astern Behind (used to describe position outside the boat).

Back To set a sail on the 'wrong' side of the boat, or to allow it to fill from the 'wrong' side.

Battens Stiffening pieces, usually of wood or glassfibre, used to support the leech of a sail.

Bear away To alter course away from the wind.

Bear off To push off, eg from a jetty or other boat.

Beat That part of the course which is in an upwind direction.

Beating Sailing towards the direction from which the wind is blowing by tacking first one way, then the other.

Block Pulley used to route a rope, wire or control line.

Bolt rope Rope stitched into the edge of a sail to stop fraying, or, more usually, to hold sail in a groove on mast or boom.

Boom Horizontal spar used to extend the foot of the sail.

Bow The front end of a boat.

Burgee Small flag flown at the masthead used to indicate the owner's club (if it angular) or when the dinghy is racing square, when strictly speaking it is not burgee but a flag).

Centreboard Pivoting board set fore-and aft, which can be lowered to give later resistance to prevent the dinghy bein blown sideways.

Centreboard case Box-like structure which the centreboard is housed.

Centreplate Metal centreboard.

Cleat Fitting to which a rope may b secured.

Clew Lower aft corner of sail.

Close hauled Sailing as close to the wind possible.

Fairlead Fitting through which a line passed.

Full-and-by Sailing close hauled but wi sails full, the course being altered as th wind direction changes.

Fully-battened Sail with battens runnin along its full width.

Glassfibre Generic term used to describe material composed of strands of glas threads impregnated with polyester o epoxy resin and allowed to harden.

Gooseneck Swivel joint connecting tw spars.

Guy Line used to control spinnaker boon

Gybe To alter course by turning the ster through the direction from which the win is blowing.

Halyard Line used to haul up a sail.

Helm Collective term for rudder and tille together, *not* for the helmsman.